BEGINNER'S GUIDE TO STARTING AN ETSY STICKER SHOP

How To Start Your Own Business Creating & Selling Stickers Online

BY ANN ECKHART

Table of Contents

INTRODUCTION

As a child growing up in the 1980s, I loved stickers. Actually, I was obsessed with them! My collection included a wide variety of brands, such as Lisa Frank, Mrs. Grossman's, and the highly coveted Trend Scratch & Sniff stickers. I had sticker books, binders, boxes, and bags filled with stickers of all different types. There was a toy store in the local shopping mall that had rolls of stickers that you could tear off one at a time, and another store had racks of sticker packs for sale. Whenever I saw a new sticker that I wanted, I would beg my dad to buy it for me. I spent hours sticking stickers in my sticker books. And I traded stickers with friends on the elementary school playground.

It's no exaggeration to say that stickers were my life!

And now as an adult? Well, I still love stickers! Granted, I don't have the stacks of binders that I did as a child (really wish I'd kept those as they are worth a lot of money on eBay), but I can't pass up buying cute stickers when I see them.

Stickers can be found almost anywhere these days. Major craft stores like Michaels, Hobby Lobby, and JoAnn all carry a wide selection of stickers, and you can also find stickers at big box retailers like Target and Walmart. One of the best places to find stickers at a low price is Dollar Tree, where they carry all types of stickers. There are even sticker subscription services such as Pipsticks that deliver stickers right to your door every month.

Nowadays, people are using stickers for more than just crafting or collecting. They are often used in planners, with Erin Condron and Happy Planner being two popular brands. Stickers are also commonly used to decorate water bottles and laptops, and some people even put stickers on their cars as a form of personal expression.

The increasing popularity of stickers has given rise to a new industry: Etsy sticker shops. These small businesses, often run by women from their homes, have become extremely popular on the Etsy platform. My love of stickers prompted me to start my own Etsy sticker shop; and in this book, I will be teaching you how to start a sticker shop of your very own!

But what exactly is an Etsy sticker shop and which is right for you?

There are two main types of Etsy sticker shops:

Planner Sticker Shops: Planner sticker shops create and sell stickers that customers can use to organize and decorate their planners. The owners of these shops often design the stickers themselves, printing them onto sticker paper and using tools like Cricut machines to cut them out into individual stickers. They often offer a variety of themes and sets of stickers for customers to choose from.

Single Sticker Shops: Single sticker shops are businesses that sell individual stickers that customers can use to decorate items like water bottles and laptops. These stickers are usually made of vinyl so that they are waterproof. Some single sticker shop owners create their designs, while others purchase print-on-demand licenses from designers to use their ready-made graphics. While some single sticker shop owners print their stickers, the vast majority choose to outsource this task as printing and cutting hundreds if not thousands of individual stickers is extremely time-consuming.

There are many different levels and types of shops within these two categories, and often as Etsy sticker shops grow, so does their merchandise. It's not uncommon for shops that started solely selling stickers to expand into other stationery products as well as home décor pieces that feature their sticker designs. Some planner sticker shops expand to offering single stickers, too.

And that's what makes having an Etsy sticker shop so much fun: You get to decide what types of stickers you want to create and sell and how far you want to take your business!

Whichever sticker shop model you choose – planner, single, or a combination of both – in this book I'm going to teach you everything you need to know to start, run and grow a successful Etsy sticker shop, including:

- How to research what sticker designs will sell
- How to design, print, and cut stickers yourself; OR
- How to outsource the design, printing, and cutting of stickers
- How to set up your Etsy sticker shop
- How to list stickers on Etsy
- How to ship out your sticker orders
- How to market and advertise your stickers
- How to grow and expand your Etsy business
- How to manage customer service issues
- How to easily manage your shop's accounting and taxes

I'll also share with you what a typical day looks like for me in the running of my own Etsy sticker shop.

To run a profitable sticker shop on Etsy, it is important to have as much knowledge as possible about the industry. The competition on Etsy can be intense, but by following the tips outlined in this book, you can set yourself up for success and potentially even build a sticker shop empire of your very own!

I've started numerous e-commerce businesses over the years but running my Etsy sticker shop is by far the most fun I've ever had! I hope that by sharing what I've learned along the way I can inspire you to start your own Etsy shop to not only make money but also have a great time!

CHAPTER ONE: ALL ABOUT ETSY STICKER SHOPS

The history of stickers can be traced back to ancient civilizations, where people used seals to mark ownership or authenticity of documents and objects. However, the modern concept of stickers as a form of decoration and personal expression likely began in the mid-20th century with the development of peel-and-stick adhesive technology.

In the 1950s and 1960s, stickers began to be used as a marketing tool, with companies printing their logos and slogans on stickers and distributing them as promotional items. But it wasn't until the 1970s and 1980s when stickers became increasingly popular among children and young people, who used them for craft projects and as a form of personal expression, decorating items like notebooks, folders, and clothing with stickers.

Stickers transformed from basic paper decals into options with prisms, glitter, holographs, and even scents. Sticker brands such as Mrs. Grossman's, Lisa Frank, and Trend became as popular as traditional toy brands such as Mattel and Playskool. Sticker collections and sticker trading also became popular pastimes with sticker books and binders as must-have accessories for collectors. Sticker displays became the norm in toy stores, and there were even dedicated sticker shops. You could even get stickers from vending machines!

Today, stickers continue to be widely used for both business and personal use. And while simply collecting stickers isn't as popular a pastime as it was for baby boomers and GenX, stickers are now used in crafting (specifically in scrapbooking), planners, and the decoration of water bottles and laptops. Stickers now come in even more sizes and materials than ever with new themes and designs continually coming onto the market.

Although stickers can be sold on various online platforms including Amazon and eBay, many sticker shop owners choose to sell their products on Etsy. This is because Etsy is a marketplace specifically designed for small businesses and handmade or vintage items, which makes it well-suited for sticker shops. Their customizable shop pages, easy-to-use listing tools, and a built-in customer base of shoppers actively buying stickers make Etsy the number one choice for sticker shops.

Most independent sticker shops choose to start their business on Etsy, and many continue to sell on the platform even as they grow and expand to other sites, including launching their own Shopify stores. But while selling stickers on other websites can be profitable, Etsy is still the best place for starting a sticker shop.

Etsy was created to provide a platform for artists, makers, and designers to sell their handmade or vintage products. Since its founding in 2006, the platform has grown to include a wide range of categories, including crafting supplies, vintage collectibles and decor, and even digital products that customers can download.

Despite this expansion, Etsy has remained true to its roots as a marketplace for handmade and unique items, another reason why it is a popular choice for sticker shops. Stickers, with their combination of unique design and function, fit perfectly within Etsy's mission to support and showcase the work of independent creators.

Etsy provides sellers with a comprehensive website that allows them to run their businesses efficiently. One of the main benefits of selling on Etsy is the ease with which sellers can list their items for sale and manage their orders. With just a few clicks, sellers can create professional-looking listings and make them available to millions of potential customers.

Another perk is that Etsy handles all of the back-end tasks associated with selling online, such as processing customer payments, collecting and remitting state sales tax, and linking to USPS to purchase and print shipping labels. This means that sellers can focus on creating and promoting their products, rather than worrying about the technicalities of running an online store. Overall, Etsy's features and tools are the reason I choose to start my own sticker shop on the platform.

Along with a full desktop version, Etsy's convenient app makes it easy for both sellers and buyers to access the marketplace on the go. With over 82 million buyers and nearly 5 million sellers, the platform offers a wide range of products and a large customer base for sellers to tap into. This can be especially beneficial for small businesses, as it can be challenging to drive traffic to a personal website.

Etsy also has a strong track record of success, with gross consolidated sales of $4.2 billion in 2021, representing a growth of 16.5% over the previous year. This shows that buyers continue to flock to the platform, making it a viable option for sellers looking to reach a large and engaged audience.

Selling on Etsy does come at a price, however. Etsy charges fees to sellers to provide various services, including hosting and maintaining the marketplace, processing transactions, and offering tools and support to sellers.

The fees that Etsy charges are as follows:

Listing Fees: Etsy charges a fee to list an item for sale on the platform. This fee is $0.20 per item, and it is charged when a seller creates a new listing or relists an expired one. The $.20 listing fee is for four months;

at the end of four months, you can choose to have the listing renewed for an additional four months at another $.20. This means that it will only cost you $.80 to keep one listing active on Etsy for an entire year, which is an incredibly affordable price!

Transaction Fees: Etsy charges a transaction fee on each sale that is made through the platform. This fee is 5% of the sale price, including shipping and gift-wrapping charges. This fee contributes to the cost of running the entire Etsy site, which is again a very affordable price compared to what you would pay if you have your own website.

Payment Processing Fees: Etsy partners with various payment processors to handle transactions on the platform. These processors charge a fee for their services, which is typically around 2.9% + $0.30 per transaction. This allows customers to pay for their orders using their debit cards, credit cards, or PayPal. Again, this service would cost much more if you had a stand-alone website.

Shipping Label Fees: If a seller opts to use Etsy's shipping label feature, they will be charged a fee for the label. The fee depends on the shipping service and destination, and it is calculated based on the weight and dimensions of the package. The fact that Etsy will automatically connect your shop with USPS shipping labels is a huge advantage. When a customer places an order, Etsy automatically calculates the cost of the label based on the weight of the order and where it is shipping to. There is no need to manually enter the customer's address or figure out the cost of postage.

While some people scoff at paying Etsy fees, the fact is that these charges help to cover the costs of running and maintaining the Etsy platform, and they allow sellers to focus on creating and selling their products rather than worrying about the technicalities of operating an online store.

I don't have the time, ability, or skill to develop a website, build a following, and set up payment processing – including collecting and remitting sales tax to the individual states – while also developing, listing, and shipping new stickers. I'm more than happy to pay Etsy these fees to take care of the backend of my business while I focus on the tasks I enjoy most, which is creating and selling stickers!

Advertising & Promotional Fees: In addition to the fees outlined above, Etsy offers various advertising and promotional options for sellers who want to increase the visibility of their products. These options come with additional fees, which vary depending on the specific advertising or promotion being used.

Promoted Listings: Etsy allows sellers to bid on keywords to have their products appear at the top of search results when customers search for those keywords. The cost of promoted listings is determined by the seller's bid and the competition for the keyword.

Etsy Ads: Etsy Ads is an optional pay-per-click advertising program that allows sellers to advertise their products on Etsy and other websites within the Etsy Ads network. Sellers set their daily maximum budget and bid for each click, and they are only charged when a customer clicks on their ad. This means that sellers have control over how much they spend on advertising and can adjust their budget as needed.

Etsy Ads can be a useful tool to increase the visibility of your stickers on the platform and drive more traffic to your shop. However, it is important to carefully consider the costs and benefits of using Etsy Ads before deciding to invest in them. Most sellers start with a $5 a day budget and let the ads run for one month to see if they were effective. You can start and stop ads, as well as adjust your daily budget, at any time.

Etsy Off-Site Ads: Etsy Offsite Ads is a pay-per-click advertising program that allows sellers to advertise their products on other websites and apps within the Etsy Ads network. When a customer clicks on an ad, they are redirected to the seller's product page on Etsy. Sellers set their budget and bid for each click, and they only pay when a customer clicks on their ad.

Etsy Offsite Ads can be a useful tool for sellers who want to increase the visibility of their products beyond the Etsy platform. By targeting ads to specific audiences and locations, sellers can reach new customers who may not have discovered their products on Etsy. However, it is important to carefully consider the costs and benefits of using Offsite Ads, as they may not always be the most cost-effective way to advertise. Sellers should also be aware that Offsite Ads are separate from Promoted Listings and Etsy Ads discussed previously.

While Etsy Offsite Ads is an optional advertising program for shops that sell less than $10,000 in 365 days, sellers who sell more than $10,000 in 365 days are automatically enrolled in the program and are required to participate. This is because Etsy Offsite Ads are one of the ways that the company generates revenue to cover the costs of operating and maintaining the platform. However, sellers only pay when an ad leads to a sale.

We will discuss Etsy Ads more in-depth later on in this book.

Payment Processing: A huge issue many people face when starting a business is how to accept payments. When I first started selling online on eBay in 2005, some customers mailed me checks and even cash to pay for their items! Fortunately, most online selling platforms, including Etsy, handle payments for sellers, meaning you don't have to worry about collecting money from your customers. Etsy handles all of that for you.

Etsy's payment processing service is called Etsy Payments, and it allows sellers to accept payment from buyers through a variety of methods, including credit and debit cards, PayPal, and gift cards. When a buyer places an order on Etsy, their payment is processed and held in escrow until the seller confirms that the order has been shipped. Sellers never have to send an invoice or nag a customer to pay; everything is done automatically through Etsy.

To use Etsy Payments, sellers must sign up for the service and link a bank account to their Etsy account. Sellers can then specify which payment methods they accept in their shop settings. When a buyer places an order, the payment is processed and deposited to the seller's Etsy account, minus any applicable fees. Then Etsy transfers that money to the seller's bank account.

Etsy charges a transaction fee for each sale made through the platform, which is typically a percentage of the sale price plus a fixed fee. This fee covers the cost of processing the payment and other services provided by Etsy, such as hosting the seller's shop and providing customer support. All fees and shipping charges are automatically deducted from a seller's account, meaning there is never an outstanding bill to pay.

Etsy Standard: Etsy Standard is the basic level of service that is available to all sellers on the platform. With Etsy Standard, sellers can create an account, which automatically creates an Etsy shop, list items for sale, and customize their shop page. The listing fee for Etsy Standard is $0.20 per item for a four-month period, and this fee is charged when a seller creates a new listing or relists an expired one.

Etsy Standard also includes various tools and features to help sellers manage their shops and reach customers, such as customizable shop pages, easy-to-use listing tools, and integration with social media. Overall, Etsy Standard provides sellers with a comprehensive set of tools and features to help them get started on the platform and start making sales.

Etsy Plus: Etsy Plus is a paid subscription plan that offers additional features and tools for sellers on the platform. For $10 a month, in addition to the features included with Etsy Standard, Etsy Plus provides sellers with a monthly budget of 15 credits for listings and $5 for Etsy Ads. These credits can be used to promote listings through the Promoted Listings and Etsy Ads programs.

Etsy Plus also includes various other benefits, such as enhanced shop appearance, a custom domain name, and access to Etsy's wholesale platform. Additionally, Etsy Plus subscribers receive a discount on Hover domains through Etsy. However, it is also possible for sellers to purchase a domain from other providers, such as GoDaddy if they prefer. Overall, purchasing a custom domain can be a useful tool for sellers who want to increase the visibility and professionalism of their Etsy shop.

Advanced Shop Customization: One of the main benefits of an Etsy Plus subscription is the ability to customize the appearance of a seller's shop page. With Advanced Shop Customization, sellers can make their Etsy shop more visually appealing and more closely align it with their brand. Some of the ways that sellers can customize their shop page with an Etsy Plus subscription include:

Custom Banner: All Etsy sellers have the option to display a banner image at the top of their shop page, which can be used to create a visually appealing and branded introduction to their shop. There are two types of banners available to all sellers: a mini banner, which is a small square image, and a big banner, which is a larger rectangular image.

Etsy Plus subscribers have the option to use more advanced banner types, such as a carousel banner and a collage banner. A carousel banner allows sellers to display up to four different images that shoppers can scroll through, and it can also include a banner image that links to a specific listing or shop section. A collage banner allows sellers to create a banner using two, three, or four different images.

Custom Avatar: A custom avatar, often referred to as a "profile picture," is a small image that represents a seller's shop on Etsy and other platforms, such as social media. You want to upload a custom avatar image or else that space will appear blank. Most shops use their business logo as their custom avatar.

Custom Shop Announcement: A custom shop announcement is a message that appears at the top of a seller's shop page on Etsy. Sellers can use this feature to announce promotions, new products, or other important updates to their customers. You can create a custom shop announcement by accessing the "Shop Manager" section of your account and clicking on the "Announcement" tab. From there, you can enter the text of your announcement and choose when it should be displayed. Note that you can edit or delete your announcement at any time.

Custom Shop Policies: Custom shop policies are a set of guidelines that outline the terms and conditions of a seller's business on Etsy. These policies can include information about returns and exchanges, shipping policies, privacy policies, and other important details.

You can create your custom shop policies by accessing the "Shop Manager" section of your account and clicking on the "Policies" tab. From there, you can create or edit your shop policies by entering the relevant information and saving their changes. It is important to carefully consider the content of your custom shop policies to ensure that they are thorough, clear, and accurate and that they meet any legal requirements.

Featured Items: Featured items are listings or shop sections that are prominently displayed on a seller's shop page. All sellers on Etsy have the option to feature up to four listings or shop sections on their shop page, which can help highlight specific products or categories.

Etsy Plus subscribers have the additional option to use a mixed grid layout, which allows them to feature one large listing or shop section along with four small items or shop sections. This layout option can be a useful way for sellers to showcase a variety of products or categories to entice customers to add similar items to their orders.

To feature items on your shop page, access the "Shop Manager" section of your account and click on the "Listings" or "Shop sections" tab. From there, select the items or sections you want to feature and use the "Feature on shop" option to add them to the featured items section of your shop page. It is important to carefully consider the items or sections you choose to feature, as these items will be prominently displayed to shoppers and may influence their decision to purchase.

Discounts & Perks: Etsy Plus subscribers have access to various discounts and perks that can help them save money and grow their business. One of the perks available to Etsy Plus subscribers is a discount on marketing materials from Moo, a company that provides high-quality printing and design services for businesses. Etsy Plus subscribers can save up to 30% on marketing materials from Moo, such as business cards, flyers, and postcards.

Another perk available to Etsy Plus subscribers is a discount on custom packaging from BoxUp, a company that specializes in custom packaging solutions for businesses. Etsy Plus subscribers can save up to 20% on custom packaging from BoxUp, which can help create a professional and branded experience for their customers.

Should you start your Etsy sticker shop with Etsy Standard or upgrade to Etsy Plus? I subscribe to Etsy Plus for my sticker shop. The listing and ad credits, the customization options, the advanced shop management, and promotional tools, and the priority customer support, to me, are all well worth the $10 monthly fee. However, you can start with Etsy Standard and upgrade to Etsy Plus if you prefer.

Sales Tax: One of the biggest benefits of selling on Etsy is that the platform handles the collection and remittance of state sales tax on behalf of sellers. This can be a significant burden for many sellers, as most American states require customers to pay sales tax on online orders and mandate that sellers remit this tax to each of the states individually. However, Etsy takes care of this process for its sellers. This is a huge perk of selling on Etsy versus selling via your website and is one of the biggest reasons sellers shy away from starting their own Shopify stores, instead choosing to keep their sticker shops on Etsy.

Seller Protection: Etsy provides several protections for sellers on its platform, including:

Payment Protection: Etsy offers payment protection for sellers through its Etsy Payments service. This means that buyers' payments are held in escrow until the seller confirms that the order has been shipped. Sellers don't have to worry about collecting payment from customers; Etsy handles this for us.

Dispute Resolution: If a seller has an issue with a buyer, they can use Etsy's dispute resolution process to try to resolve the issue. This can include mediation, where Etsy will help facilitate communication between the seller and buyer, or arbitration, where Etsy will make a final decision on the dispute. Note that buyers can also use this service if they are having issues with a seller.

Seller Protection Insurance: Etsy offers seller protection insurance to eligible sellers in certain countries, which can provide coverage for lost or damaged items and other issues that may arise during the shipping process.

Overall, these protections are in place to help ensure that sellers can sell on Etsy with confidence and minimize the risk of issues arising during the buying and selling process.

Why would you start your sticker shop on Etsy? The question is, why wouldn't you? With a large customer base, an easy-to-use platform, and financials managed for you, Etsy is definitely the best place to start a sticker shop!

CHAPTER TWO: RESEARCHING PROFITABLE STICKER DESIGNS & TRENDS

You now know why Etsy is the best place to start a sticker shop. And you may already know if you want to sell planner stickers or individual stickers. But what about the design of your stickers? After all, there are hundreds of different themes stickers fall under, including:

- Pop culture
- Animals
- Food
- Holidays
- Special Occasions
- Nature
- Humor
- Travel
- Sports
- Politics
- Art

The possibilities for sticker designs are endless. But before you design your first sticker, there are some things you need to know.

Trademark Infringement: Trademark infringement is something you must be aware of before you list any stickers for sale. Trademark law protects words, phrases, symbols, or designs that are used to identify and distinguish a particular brand or product. If you use a trademarked term or image on your stickers without permission, you may be accused of trademark infringement, which can at the very least Etsy pulling your listing; and at worst, the company that holds the trademark suing you.

It is shocking to me how many people do not know about trademark infringement. Yet every day, Etsy Facebook groups and other online Etsy forums are filled with posts from sellers who have had their listings pulled, or worse, their accounts terminated because they violated a trademark.

So how do you know what is trademarked and what isn't?

The first step to identifying trademarks is to ask yourself if someone else created the design. Movies, music, books, actors, singers, writers, television shows, song lyrics, and quotes are almost all trademarked. If someone else wrote it, sang it, or made it, it was likely trademarked. And if something is trademarked, you cannot use it.

To avoid trademark infringement, it's important to do your research and make sure that you are not using any trademarked terms or images on your stickers without permission. You can search for registered trademarks in the US through the US Patent and Trademark Office's online database at uspto.gov/trademarks/search.

One of the biggest themes you will see on Etsy is handmade Disney products. From clothing and décor to stickers and stationery, there are thousands of Disney-themed products for sale on Etsy. However, these are all in violation of the trademark as only Disney is authorized to create and sell Disney products. Unless a seller has gotten express written permission from Disney to sell designs based on the Mouse, they are violating Disney's trademark.

But wait, I know what you are about to say: If these Disney products violate the trademark, how are sellers getting away with selling them?

The fact is that Etsy will rarely pull an item due to trademark infringement on its own. Instead, they wait until the trademark owner alerts them to listings. Disney periodically will go through the site and tell Etsy to take down listings. So, some sellers will go for quite a while selling Disney-looking items. Eventually, however, those listings will be pulled.

Etsy generally has a "three strikes and you're out" policy. If you rack up three trademark violations, Etsy will usually terminate your account. And once your account is terminated, it is gone forever. You cannot create a new selling account as you have to register using your identity and whatever government issue ID you have in your country (in America, this will be your social security account).

You may be thinking that you can simply create designs that are similar but not exactly like trademarked brands. But a company such as Disney has thousands of trademarks that cover everything from the shape of Mickey Mouse's ears to random messages that play in the theme parks. Many Disney-themed shops will say their products are Disney-inspired. But it doesn't matter; they are still violating Disney's trademark.

Violating another company's trademark is the fastest way to lose your sticker business before you even sell one item. Ignore the fact that other sellers are violating the rules and instead make sure you aren't!

So, if you can't sell Disney-themed or other pop culture-inspired stickers, what kinds of stickers can you sell? After all, aren't most things trademarked?

The answer is no, most designs aren't trademarked. You just need to be creative in the types of themes you offer. You can't use Disney designs, but you can create travel and vacation-themed stickers. You can't use quotes from songs, but you can come up with your unique sayings. You can't use a celebrity's image, but you can create your characters.

My sticker shop focus on retro and vintage designs. I offer everything from 80's inspired holographic stickers to stickers featuring mid-century modern elements. None of these objects or eras are trademarked. And if I want to use a saying or phrase, I research it to make sure it is not trademarked. Stickers are a creative business; there are endless opportunities for you to develop original designs that don't involve copying someone else.

Research: If you are an artist who wants to turn your designs into stickers, you may already have a good understanding of the types of stickers you want to sell on Etsy. However, it is still important to research the market and get a sense of what is trending to ensure that your stickers will be appealing to shoppers. You may love designing flower stickers, for example; but knowing which flower stickers are the most sought after – say, sunflowers versus roses - will give you a leg up on the competition.

On the other hand, if you are someone who just loves stickers and wants to start a business selling them, you may need to purchase graphics and outsource the printing. In this case, it is especially important to do your research to identify opportunities to create stickers that will sell well and generate income.

But how do you go about researching sticker trends and figuring out what exactly Etsy customers are looking for?

The first and easiest way to research current sticker trends on Etsy is to simply type keywords such as "stickers," "planner stickers," or "vinyl stickers" into the search bar and browse the results. And you'll want to check out the top sticker shops on the site, including:

- Planner Kate
- Doodlebug Design Inc.
- Lemonade Market
- Sticker Planet
- The Sticker Club
- Sweet Sticker Co.

Searching for stickers on Etsy as well as looking at successful sticker shops will help you see not only what themes of stickers are popular but also the current popular aesthetics. Remember that trends come and go; what is in demand one month may fall out of favor the next. When you run an Etsy sticker shop, you'll need to be on top of trends, meaning you'll want to frequently perform searches and check in on other shops.

Note that when you search on Etsy you can also use the filters on the left side of the search result's page to narrow down the results by category, price, color, and other factors. This can help you get a better understanding of the types of stickers that are selling well and identify opportunities to create products that are similar or complementary.

For example, perhaps a search for planner stickers shows that the top sellers feature stickers for moms to use when organizing their children's activities. How can you niche this category of stickers down? Maybe you could create planner stickers for single moms, planner stickers for moms who are also teachers or nurses, planner stickers for homeschool moms, or planner stickers for moms of teenagers.

Being able to target various niches is key to attracting customers on Etsy. It's nearly impossible to compete directly with the top sticker shops that have been selling products for years. However, by figuring out where there are holes in the market, you can bring something new and exciting to the site.

Another way to research current sticker trends on Etsy is to pay attention to the tags and titles that sellers use to describe their stickers. By looking at the tags and titles of popular stickers, you can get a sense of the keywords and terms that shoppers are using to find stickers on the platform. You can also use these keywords and terms to optimize the titles and tags of your stickers to make them more discoverable by shoppers.

As I sit here typing these very words, I am also running searches on Etsy to give you some examples. Note that these search results change daily based on the market, but right how when I do a simple search for "stickers," nearly 4 million results come up.

You read that right: FOUR MILLION!

That's an awful lot of listings to look at. Fortunately, Etsy offers filters you can use to narrow down your search. Playing around with these search filters is a free and easy way to learn what is currently selling.

Etsy filters are as follows:

Category: Users can filter search results by categories, such as art and collectibles, clothing and accessories, home and living, and more.

On Etsy, stickers are typically listed under the "Paper and Party Supplies" category, which includes a variety of paper-based products such as invitations, envelopes, business cards, and more. Within this category, stickers can be found in the "Stickers" subcategory, which includes a wide range of stickers for various purposes such as crafting, labeling, and decorating.

However, it is important to note that stickers may also be listed in other categories on Etsy, depending on their intended use or the materials they are made from. For example, stickers that are designed specifically for use in a planner or journal might be listed under the "Office and School Supplies" category, while stickers made from vinyl or other durable materials might be listed under the "Arts, Crafts and Sewing" category.

PRO TIP: Even if all of your stickers seem to fall within one category, try mixing it up a bit by listing some of your products, especially ones that are slower to sell, in other categories. This will help you cast a wider net on Etsy and may attract customers who aren't finding you in the main sticker category. And by listing stickers that aren't selling well in these other categories, you aren't risking your best sellers.

Price: Etsy allows users to filter search results by price ranges, such as "under $10," "$10-$25," "$25-$50," and more. Stickers are typically a lower-cost item. Even if you plan on offering higher-priced sticker sheets or collections in your shop, consider offering some low-priced options that will show up in the "under $10" filter as that will bring customers to your store who may go on to purchase higher-dollar items from you.

Color: Etsy users can filter search results by color, such as red, blue, green, and more. Sellers can select up to two colors, including rainbow, in their listings. You want to fill out the color fields for your stickers to give your products a better chance of being found in search. If you have stickers with multiple colors in them, choose the most prominent colors or select "rainbow."

Shipping Location: Customers can filter search results by the location where the item is shipped from, such as the United States, the United Kingdom, or Canada. I personally only ship to customers in the United States, but this is a personal decision. Opening your shop up to international orders can help increase your sales.

Note that you can offer "free" shipping to customers within your own country but charge shipping for international orders. Since international shipping costs are very high, this is a good way to manage costs. Many international customers will be turned off by the high cost of postage, but you might be surprised by how many people will pay the extra postage price if they find an item they want.

Material: Etsy shoppers can filter search results by the materials used to create the item, such as wood, metal, ceramic, and paper. Most stickers are either paper or vinyl. While "paper" is sometimes listed as a material option in some categories, it isn't always. And vinyl is never listed as an option.

Occasion: Etsy allows users to filter search results by occasion, such as birthdays, weddings, baby showers, and other special events. When you are creating your sticker listings, the occasions available for you to select will vary depending on the category you are listing the item under. I rarely choose an occasion for my sticker listings as my stickers are typically for everyday use or holiday (i.e., Halloween, Christmas, Easter), not a particular event (graduation, baptism, retirement).

Era: Shoppers can filter search results by era, such as vintage (at least 20 years old), antique (at least 100 years old), or current. If you are making your stickers, then you'll be listing them as the current year. Because stickers are considered a handmade item as well as a supply to make things (planner stickers to use in planners, vinyl stickers for decorating water bottles), stickers fall under two of Etsy's three categories (vintage, handmade, supply).

Gift Wrapping: Etsy allows users to filter search results by whether the seller offers gift wrapping. While Etsy is known as a website where people shop for gifts, and while I have had some customers send my stickers as gifts, gift wrapping isn't something that sticker shops typically offer. Unless you are making stickers that are specifically meant to be given as gifts, customers are not going to expect you to gift wrap them. Etsy allows customers to mark orders as gifts and to have their orders include a gift slip with a personalized note.

Special Offers: Etsy offers shoppers a "Special Offers" filter that users can select to narrow down search results to items that are on sale or have other special deals available. To use the special offers filter, you can simply click on the "Special Offers" option in the "Price" section of the filters on the left side of the search results page. This will display only the items that have special offers available, such as sale items, bulk discounts, or gifts with purchase.

Keep in mind that the availability and terms of special offers may vary depending on the seller and the item being offered. Some sellers may offer discounts on certain items or categories as a promotion or to clear out inventory, while others may offer special deals or bundles for a limited time. Make sure you read an item's description and the seller's policies before purchasing to understand the terms and conditions of the special offers available. As a seller, make sure your policies regarding offers are clear, too.

Estimated Arrival: Online shoppers expect their orders to arrive quickly. But with Etsy being known for handmade items, shoppers also know that custom orders take more time. The ability to filter search results based on the estimated arrival time brings the shops that offer the fastest shipping to the top. I ship all of my orders the following business day, and I suggest you offer one-to-two-day shipping, too, to be competitive. When price and design are the same, a customer will next choose the speed of shipping when deciding which shop to buy from.

Holiday: Etsy's "Holiday" filter includes a range of holidays that users can select from to narrow down search results. Note that the holidays available depend on the category the item was listed in. For example, the holidays available for sticker listings may differ from the coffee mug listings. As with the occasion filter, you may not find a holiday to list your stickers under; and that is okay.

The filters that you use on Etsy can significantly impact the number of search results that you see, as they allow you to narrow down the results to only show items that meet certain criteria. For example, using the "Christmas" and "Red" filters would significantly narrow down the search results, resulting in fewer listings being shown. However, if you remove those filters and only use "Bestseller" and "United States," the number of search results increases significantly, as those filters are less restrictive.

Using the filters on Etsy can be a helpful way to get a sense of what types of stickers are currently being offered on the platform and identify any gaps in the market that you could potentially fill with your designs. By experimenting with different combinations of filters and paying attention to the search results, you can get a sense of what types of stickers are popular, what materials and techniques are being used, and what price points are typical for similar items.

In addition to using the filters, you can also **browse through the different categories and subcategories on Etsy** to see what types of stickers are being sold in each area. What is popular for planner stickers may be vastly different from the best-selling vinyl stickers, which customers put on water bottles and laptops. This is why it's important to make sure you are researching not only the designs of stickers but also the categories they are in. You may find that shoppers simply aren't buying the stickers you want to offer. But you might stumble upon popular themes you never even thought about.

Visiting craft stores and other retailers in your area can be a helpful way to get a sense of what types of stickers are currently popular and in demand, as well as identify any gaps in the market that you could potentially fill with your designs. By looking at the stickers that are being sold at these stores, you can get a sense of the materials, techniques, and themes that are being used, and use this information to inform your product development.

Take note of the stickers that are low in stock, meaning customers are buying them. Also look at the stickers that are on clearance, as those are stickers customers aren't buying. What are the popular designs that the store is having trouble keeping in stock? What are the stickers they can't seem to get rid of? Noting what isn't selling is just as important – and maybe more so – than seeing what is selling.

As always, remember that you want to avoid copying the designs of other sellers or retailers, as this could result in legal issues. Instead, try to use what you see as inspiration to come up with your unique ideas and concepts. As I've already discussed, you aren't going to be able to go head-to-head with the big stationery companies or even the top Etsy shops. But you can look to them for inspiration on niches they aren't covering.

In addition to going into the brick-and-mortar stores, check out their websites as you will be able to read reviews of the products. Note what customers have to say about the stickers they purchased. What did they like? What didn't they like? How do they wish the product was different? You can learn a lot about what works and what doesn't from these reviews and apply the feedback to your products.

By specializing in your sticker offerings and targeting a specific niche, you will be more likely to identify and fill a void in the market, as well as command higher prices for your products. While basic planner stickers are readily available, offering specialized stickers designed for a particular group of people can give you an edge in the market. By focusing on a specific niche, you can create stickers that are more tailored to the needs and interests of your target audience, which can help you stand out from the competition and attract loyal customers.

Think of all of the different ways people characterize themselves, including:

- Gender
- Age
- Sexuality
- Relationship status

- Hometown
- Current location
- Pets
- Family
- Religion
- Politics
- Education
- Career
- Hobbies
- Interests
- Personality traits

How can you create stickers that target these different niches? A 50-something nurse living in Ohio whose children are now in college and who loves cats, crafting, and travel is a much different customer than a 20-something college student originally from California who is currently studying to be a doctor in New York. The way these two individuals use planners is likely very different. How could you design planner stickers that would meet their needs?

Vinyl stickers cater to a much different customer than planner stickers. When creating individual vinyl stickers, it's important to conduct thorough research to understand the market and identify any gaps that you could potentially fill with your designs. As with planner stickers, this can include using the filters on Etsy to explore different types of stickers and see what is currently being offered, as well as looking at stickers being sold in physical stores to get a sense of current trends and customer preferences.

It can also be helpful to consider your interests and hobbies, as well as your lifestyle, to see if there are any areas where you feel that you could contribute unique or specialized designs. If you are a gardener, for example, you likely love plants and flowers. Botanical vinyl stickers are very popular and are a great niche to target. Or maybe you are in the medical field. Doctors, nurses, and other healthcare professionals often carry water bottles during their workdays. What are some fun sayings that you and your co-workers use that you could turn into stickers?

Google Trends: In addition to using Etsy to research stickers, you can also use Google Trends, which is a free tool that allows you to see how often specific keywords or phrases are being searched for on Google over time. You can use this tool to track the popularity of specific types of products or themes on Etsy and see how demand for these items has changed over time.

To use Google Trends to research popular Etsy sticker shops, follow these steps:

1. Go to the Google Trends website at trends.google.com.
2. In the "Search for a topic" field, enter "stickers," "planner stickers," or "vinyl stickers" (or play around with all three search terms)
3. In the "Location" field, select the country or region that you are interested in researching.
4. 4. In the "Time range" field, select the time that you want to analyze.
5. 5. Click the "Go" button.

You will be shown a graph displaying the popularity of the search term you entered over time in the location and period that you specified. For instance, if you search for "stickers' around December, you will see that Christmas stickers are the most searched.

What I like to see in this Google Trend search is from which states customers are the most interested in stickers. For example, on the day of writing this section of this book, the top results were South Dakota, Delaware, Alaska, Missouri, and Idaho. What stickers can you create for these customers? What is special about each of these states? A search of "South Dakota stickers" on Etsy will show you what other shops are selling. What can you do that is different?

While noting where sticker shoppers are located is great data to have, even better is to know exactly what they are searching for. That is where **Trending Searches** come in. You can find the Trending Searches option on the left-hand side of the Google Trends page.

Trending Searches isn't going to show you what stickers people are searching for. Rather, it will show you what topics people are currently searching the internet for. This will help you identify popular topics that you could potentially create stickers around.

It's important to note that most of the trends will be for trademarked products such as sports teams, movies, and songs. And while we've already established that you cannot create and sell stickers that use trademarked images or words, you can gain inspiration from these trends.

Seeing what music artists are popular could help you develop stickers for genres of music, for example. Or if you see sports teams trending, think about what stickers you could develop around the sport itself, not the trademarked team.

Pinterest: Pinterest is a social media platform that allows users to create and share collections of images and ideas. You can use Pinterest to search for specific types of products or themes and see what other users are pinning and sharing. This can give you a sense of what types of products are popular and inspire your product development.

To use Pinterest to research sticker trends:

1. Go to the Pinterest website (https://www.pinterest.com/) and create an account if you don't already have one. I will

discuss using Pinterest to promote your Etsy sticker shop later in this book, so go ahead and create an account now as you will want to use the site to attract customers. It's free and easy to do.

2. In the search bar at the top of the page, enter a relevant search term, such as "sticker trends" or "sticker design ideas."
3. Click the "Search" button.
4. Scroll through the search results to see the most popular pins related to your search term.
5. Click on individual pins to see more details and to view the source of the pin.

You can also use Pinterest's "Explore" feature to discover new trends and ideas:

1. Click on the "Explore" icon (a compass) at the top of the Pinterest homepage.
2. Scroll through the "Explore" feed to see popular pins and boards related to your interests.
3. Click on individual pins or boards to see more details and to view the source of the pin or board.

Pinterest can be a useful tool for researching sticker trends because it allows you to see what designs and ideas are popular among Pinterest users. You can use the search and explore features to find inspiration and ideas for your stickers and to see what is currently popular on the platform. Keep in mind that the popularity of certain trends may vary based on the location and audience of the users who are using Pinterest.

Don't just look at the Pinterest results, create your own boards to save and share designs you like. This will help you connect with others in the sticker community and to build a potential customer base for when you launch your stickers. Following other Pinterest users and boards is a free and easy way to interact with other users on the platform, some of whom may one day be your customers!

Paid Tools: Etsy, Pinterest, Google, and retail stores are free and easy ways to research sticker trends. However, there are several third-party tools available that can be useful for researching and analyzing products and trends on Etsy, including stickers. These tools can provide insights into things like sales history, search ranking, and competition within specific niches.

Using a paid tool isn't a requirement for building a successful Etsy shop, but it can come in handy, especially if you have no idea of the types of stickers you want to sell. Most of these sites offer free trials and then month-to-month subscriptions so that you can test them out before deciding if you want to commit to a yearly plan. While you will save money when you commit to a yearly subscription, it's best to test these sites out for a month at a time before deciding if the cost is worth it.

Some examples of paid third-party tools for Etsy research include:

eRank.com: This tool allows you to see the search ranking of specific keywords and products on Etsy. It can help you understand how your products and keywords are performing on the platform and how they compare to other sellers.

I use eRank for researching sticker trends on Etsy. I have a Pro subscription, and I have my own Etsy shop synced so that I can get customized data. By typing keywords into eRank's search bar, the site will show you what customers are shopping for and what the competition for that keyword is.

PRO TIP: Look for trends that have a high search rank but a low competition rank. Remember that Etsy is very competitive. You must seek out underserved markets to attract buyers. On the day I am writing this section, typing "stickers' into the search bar gives me dozens of results. I notice that one result is "frog stickers," which has a very high rate of searches but a low number of competing shops. If I were looking for new stickers to make, I would add "frog stickers" to my list as there is an opportunity to fill a niche.

Note that you will see trademarked results show up on all these Etsy research tools, including eRank. For example, Taylor Swift, Harry Potter, and Star Wars all appear high on the list of trending stickers. Remember, however, that these are licensed names that you cannot use. Yes, other sellers may be selling these trademarked products now, but it's only a matter of time before their listings are pulled.

Etsycheck.com: Etsy Check is another tool that allows you to see the sales history and search ranking of specific products on Etsy. Its interface is simpler than eRank's and you don't get the in-depth data that eRank provides, especially when it comes to researching trends. I use it to find keywords, specifically for use in tags, for my Etsy sticker shop.

When I am creating an Etsy sticker listing, I will log into Etsy Check, use the tag generator, and search for the item I am listing. For example, if I am listing a Christmas sticker, I will type "Christmas sticker" into the search bar. As with eRank, the results will show the competition for a particular keyword. For example, "Christmas stickers" has the highest level of competition. However, "Xmas stickers" has a much lower level of competition. This data would tell me that I should add "Xmas stickers" to my title and tags. It would also allow me to create stickers that say "Xmas" rather than "Christmas."

Everbee.io: This tool allows you to research and analyze products on Etsy to identify trends and opportunities within specific niches. It can help you identify products that are performing well within a specific niche and find inspiration for new products. As with eRank, you can connect your Etsy shop to Everbee. Everbee is very similar to eRank in that it is a great way to research trends. Most Etsy sellers use eRank or Everbee, not both. Both have a free trial you can sign up for before you decide if you want to pay for a subscription.

Using paid third-party tools for Etsy research can be useful for sellers who do not want to do the leg work of researching sticker trends directly on Etsy or other websites. I use eRank for research and Etsy Check for generating tags and keywords. It is important to note that these tools are not affiliated with Etsy and the results they provide may not always be accurate. As such, it is important to use these tools as a guide rather than a definitive source of information. At the end of the day, you will only know how sellable your products are after they have been listed for sale.

I entered into starting an Etsy shop knowing that I wanted to sell vintage and retro-inspired stickers. I didn't start to use paid tools until several months into selling on Etsy. These paid tools aren't a necessity for starting an Etsy sticker shop, but they can offer some help if you have no idea where to start researching trends or finding keywords and tags.

CHAPTER THREE: CHOOSING YOUR STICKER SHOP BUSINESS MODEL

As we've already discussed, there are many different types of Etsy sticker shops, as stickers can be made for a wide range of purposes and can be customized to suit various needs. Some popular types of stickers along with common Etsy sticker shops include:

Scrapbooking Stickers: These stickers are designed for use in scrapbooking and other paper crafts. They can include a wide range of themes, such as holidays, birthdays, and special occasions. Numbers, letters, and phrases are the most common types of scrapbook stickers and they almost always come on sheets.

Planner Stickers: These stickers are designed for use in planners, agendas, and journals. They can include a wide range of themes, such as daily tasks, appointments, and reminders. Two of the largest planner sticker companies are Erin Condren and Happy Planner, both of which have websites you can browse to get an idea of what planner stickers are currently on the market. As with scrapbooking stickers, most planner stickers come in sheets.

Decorative Stickers: These stickers are designed for use as decorations on wrapped gifts, book covers, and even windows and walls. Decorative stickers can include a wide range of themes, such as animals, flowers, and geometric patterns. Decorative stickers can be paper or vinyl and can come in sheets or as singles. Vinyl stickers that people put on water bottles and laptops can also be referred to as decorative stickers.

Personalized Stickers: These stickers are customized with a name or other personal information. They can be used for a variety of purposes, such as labeling school supplies or personalizing gifts. Personalized stickers are a great niche item to sell on Etsy as they are in demand but there aren't as many shops offering them. Typically shops that offer personalized stickers are designing, printing, and cutting the stickers in-house.

A quick search of "personalized stickers" on Etsy will show you the top sellers in this niche, which are custom stickers for businesses and custom children's name stickers. However, some shops offer personalized stickers for party favors, wedding favors, and family events. Selling personalized stickers is the most time-consuming sticker shop model as every order needs to be customized. Because of this, it can also cause the most customer service issues due to misspellings or stickers being ordered for an event that arrives late.

Sticker Sets: These are collections of stickers that are themed around a particular subject or interest, such as animals, nature, or popular culture. Sticker sets can also fall under scrapbook stickers and planner stickers. Many planner sticker shops offer sticker sets in various themes. But even shops that typically focus on single stickers might add some sticker sheets to their shop as a way to diversify and attract new customers. While many Etsy sticker shops print their sticker sheets in-house, websites such as StickerMule can print sticker sheets for you of the designs you upload. And there are print-on-demand providers, including Printify and Printful, who will print and ship your stickers sheets directly to your customers.

Die-Cut Stickers: These stickers are cut into specific shapes (i.e., not simply round or square) and can be used for a variety of purposes, such as labeling items or decorating surfaces. Die-cut stickers can be used in scrapbooks, planners, and, if printed on waterproof vinyl, on water bottles. Most customers expect personalized name stickers to be die-cut. If you plan to print your stickers, you will need a cutting machine to die-cut them. Or companies such as StickerMule can print and cut die-cut stickers for you.

Transparent Stickers: Transparent stickers, also referred to as "clear stickers," are made from transparent material and can be used to add a decorative element to windows or other surfaces without obscuring the view. A transparent sticker showcases the graphic without a background. If you plan to print your stickers but don't have a cutting machine, transparent stickers are a good option as you don't need to cut around the image.

Waterproof Stickers: These stickers, also commonly referred to as "vinyl stickers," are made from waterproof material and can be used to label items or decorate surfaces that may encounter water. Waterproof stickers are extremely popular as customers use them to decorate water bottles. The second most common use for vinyl stickers is to put them on laptops. Since vinyl stickers are also typically heat-safe, they can withstand the heat computers generate.

Vinyl sticker paper is available if you plan to print and cut your stickers; otherwise, there are numerous sticker printing companies (I use StickerMule), including print-on-demand companies (Printify is the most popular), that can print vinyl stickers for you.

The two most common sticker shop models are **Planner Sticker Shops** (which usually include sticker sheets) and **Vinyl Sticker Shops** (individual waterproof stickers that are safe for water bottles and laptops). Many of the stickers listed above can also fall into these sticker shop models. For instance, I sell vinyl stickers. While most people use vinyl stickers to decorate water bottles and laptops, they can also be used in crafting and decorating.

Planner Sticker Shops: Planners (also referred to as "agendas" in some areas) and planner accessories are a big business. Every year, hundreds of millions of people purchase planners and then seek out accessories to decorate and organize the pages. Etsy planner sticker shops offer a wide range of planner stickers to suit different planning needs and styles. Successful planner sticker shops are continually offering new designs and themes to keep customers coming back for the latest offerings.

The vast majority of planner sticker shops design, print, and cut their stickers in-house. This involves designing the stickers using graphic design software, printing the stickers out onto sticker paper, and then using a cutting machine to perforate between the stickers so that users can peel them off.

Most Etsy planner sticker shops begin by offering one type of planner sticker and then adding other stickers. Some common types of planner stickers that an Etsy shop might offer include:

Daily Planner Stickers: Daily planner stickers are designed to mark specific tasks or events daily. They can include a wide range of themes, such as to-do lists, appointments, and reminders. Daily planner stickers are typically sheets of stickers with numerous options available on one sheet. For example, a daily planner sticker sheet might include different colors and fonts, allowing the user to customize their pages.

"Planner addicts," as planner enthusiasts are referred to, love to use coordinating colors on their pages, meaning they are likely to buy multiple daily planner sheets to have enough to use over a month or year. Note that daily planner stickers need to be sized to fit inside calendar squares. This means that you will need to size them correctly and maybe even offer different sizes for different planners.

Weekly Planner Stickers: Weekly planner stickers are designed to mark tasks or events every week. They can include a wide range of themes, such as to-do lists, appointments, and reminders. Just like daily planner stickers, weekly planner stickers are usually printed on sheets.

However, weekly planner stickers typically have a longer duration than daily planner stickers and are used to mark tasks or events that recur weekly. Typical uses for weekly planner stickers are to note reoccurring meetings, appointments, deadlines, special events, or occasions that occur every week, such as exercise classes or weekly date nights.

Weekly planner stickers are often larger and more decorative than daily planner stickers and come in a wider range of themes and designs. For example, if a user has a mandatory work meeting every single Monday, they may want to mark that can't-miss meeting with a larger sticker versus the smaller sticker they use to note an everyday task. If you are going to sell weekly planner stickers, think about all the niches available and try to target underserved markets.

As with daily planner stickers, monthly planner stickers are often sized to fit into a planner's calendar squares. Successful shops either find a standard size to offer or sell multiple sizes based on different planners.

Monthly Planner Stickers: Monthly planner stickers are designed to mark tasks or events that occur monthly. They can include a wide range of themes, such as to-do lists, appointments, and reminders. As with weekly planner stickers, monthly planner stickers tend to be larger than daily planner stickers. After all, users want these monthly events to stand out. Household reminders, such as monthly recycling pickup and maintenance, as well as monthly appointments such as book clubs or school meetings, are just some of the examples of monthly planner sticker uses.

PRO TIP: As noted above, daily, weekly, and monthly planner stickers are typically sized to fit inside the calendar page grids on planner sheets. While you can offer multiple sizes to fit multiple planners, it is much easier to offer one universal size. If you are confused about what sizes you need, simply buy a pack of planner stickers from a company like Happy Planner or a successful Etsy sticker shop. The goal here isn't to copy the design of the stickers but instead to see exactly how to size your sticker sheets and the stickers themselves.

Special Occasion Stickers: These stickers are designed to mark special occasions, such as birthdays, holidays, and anniversaries. Not that special occasion stickers are, in name, different from holiday stickers. Special occasions are non-holiday events, not holidays that are marked by specific days that everyone observes.

An idea for personalized special occasion stickers is to create stickers for each family member's birthday that a mom could use in her planner. Offering customers the opportunity to not only put names on stickers but to choose the colors is a great way to stand out among the crowd. After all, customers turn to Etsy because they can't make personalized products themselves; so, if you are willing and able to do so, you can charge accordingly.

While it is expected that a planner sticker shop will offer special occasion stickers for all of the typical occasions (general birthdays, anniversaries, etc.), think outside of the box for other events that users want to mark in their planners, such as their pet's birthdays, specific anniversary dates (first date, first kiss, friend-anniversaries), and milestones (children's "first", the progression of music lessons, karate black belts). The more you can niche down your offerings, the more you can charge for your products.

Holiday Stickers: Holiday stickers are designed to mark date-specific events, such as Christmas, Easter, and Halloween. Unlike special occasions, which are up to each user, holidays are universal within each country, meaning they vary by country.

And right there is a way that you can target a special niche: Sell holiday stickers for different countries! While the United States observes Thanksgiving on the last Thursday in November, Canadians observe it on the second Monday in October. And when was the last time you saw a Canadian Thanksgiving sticker?

Holiday planner stickers do sell best leading up to and during each holiday season; however, you want to make sure that you have these stickers listed well before the actual holiday. It's typical to have your holiday items listed a good three months in advance of the actual date of the holiday. This will help you attract early shoppers, which will organically push your listings up as the date of the holiday gets closer. I sell the most Christmas stickers, for example, in November. By the time December rolls around, I'm starting to see Valentine's Day sales.

That's not to say that holiday stickers only sell near their holidays. Planner users buy holiday stickers year-round. If you plan to offer holiday stickers, you can either specialize in one holiday or try to cover them all. If you absolutely love Christmas and only want to offer Christmas stickers, that's fine. Just know that you will need to list a lot of options and may have most of your sales in the weeks leading up to December 25th, not year-round.

Note that there are shops that earn a full-time income just from their fourth-quarter sales. The fourth quarter refers to the last three months of the year, which is when most retailers make the majority of their money. If you do end up with the bulk of your sales occurring between October and December, you'll be able to relax and take your time creating new products the rest of the year and spend those months simply fulfilling orders. Not a bad schedule, if you ask me!

Decorative Stickers: As I mentioned earlier, decorative stickers can be the entire theme of an Etsy shop. Decorative stickers in a non-planner shop are typically large and are meant for decorating personal spaces. Decorative PLANNER stickers, however, are smaller embellishments meant to fit onto a planner page. For example, tiny flower stickers can be used to decorate a Spring planner layout.

Decorative planner stickers are usually sold in sheets. They are a nice accompaniment to other planner sticker sheets, allowing you to sell sets. Sets are where planner sticker shops can earn a lot of money as sellers can charge more for several sheets of stickers versus one sheet or a single sticker. Decorative planner sticker sheets will coordinate with the daily, weekly, monthly, occasion, and holiday stickers in an Etsy shop. This encourages shoppers to purchase multiple stickers from the same seller so that everything matches.

Note that you can build an entire Etsy shop on just decorative stickers, both for planners and scrapbooks. If you want to create sticker sheets but don't want to deal with typical planner stickers that require precision measurements and cutting, focusing on decorative sticker sheets is a great option.

Personalized Stickers: As with decorative stickers, there are entire Etsy shops that only sell personalized stickers. Personalized children's name stickers, for example, tend to be larger than typical planner stickers as parents use them for their kid's school notebooks and to decorate their rooms.

Personalized planner stickers, however, are much smaller as they need to fit on a planner page. Popular personalized planner stickers are those of family names as users can put a name sticker next to that person's appointments and birthdays. And when you think of creating family stickers, don't forget about pets. Offering personalized stickers for cats, dogs, and other animals is a great way to distinguish your Etsy sticker shop from the rest.

Sticker Sets: These are collections of stickers that are themed around a particular subject or interest, such as animals, nature, or popular culture. Most planner sticker shops offer their stickers in sets but also offer single sheets of stickers.

The best thing about selling sticker sets is that you can charge more than you would for a single sticker sheet. And as I already mentioned, planner users love to create planner pages that have a coordinating look. By designing and coordinating daily, weekly, monthly, special occasions, holidays, and decorative stickers in various themes, you'll be able to generate larger-priced orders. And if customers like your design aesthetic, they'll come back to your shop again and again.

The average price an Etsy seller charges for six basic planner sticker sheets is around $12. If that seller were to sell those sheets individually, they would only be able to charge $2 per sheet. While the profit from each sale would be the same, the real difference comes in the shipping. It would likely cost the same to ship one sticker sheet or six sticker sheets. But the cost of shipping supplies such as mailing labels, envelopes, and enclosures would eat heavily into the profits of shipping just one sticker sheet versus six.

Dot Stickers: Dot stickers, also known as bullet stickers or dot grid stickers, are a type of planner sticker that is used to mark tasks or events in a planner or journal. They are called "dot stickers" because they are typically arranged in a grid of dots, rather than being cut into a specific shape.

Dot stickers are often used in conjunction with a "dot grid" journal or planner, which is a type of notebook that has a grid of dots on each page rather than lines or blank pages. The dots provide a guide for writing and drawing and can be used to create tables, lists, and other types of content. Dot stickers can be used to mark tasks or events in a variety of ways, such as by color-coding different types of tasks or using different symbols to represent different types of events.

Some common uses for dot stickers include marking to-do lists, appointments, and reminders. Etsy planner sticker shops may offer a variety of dot stickers to suit different planning needs and styles. These can include daily, weekly, and monthly dot stickers, as well as stickers for special occasions and holidays. They can also include a variety of colors, sizes, and shapes to suit different preferences.

PRO TIP: Note that "dot grid" is referencing "bullet journals," which is trademarked. Because Etsy sellers cannot name their products "bullet journal stickers" or "bullet journal paper," they instead refer to these items as "dot grid." You can use the keyword "bullet" in your listings, but make sure you do NOT use the word "journal." I would list these types of stickers as "dot grid stickers," "dot stickers," "bullet dots," "bullet stickers," or "bullet point stickers."

Flag Stickers: Flag stickers, also known as tab stickers or index stickers, are a type of planner sticker that is used to mark specific pages or sections in a planner or journal. They are called "flag stickers" because they are shaped like small flags and can be stuck to the edge of a page or section to mark its location. Flag stickers can be used to mark specific pages or sections in a planner or journal in a variety of ways, such as by color-coding different types of tasks or using different symbols to represent different types of events.

Some common uses for flag stickers include marking to-do lists, appointments, and reminders. Etsy sticker shops may offer a variety of flag stickers to suit different planning needs and styles. These can include daily, weekly, and monthly flag stickers, as well as stickers for special occasions and holidays. They can also include a variety of colors, sizes, and shapes to suit different preferences. In addition to being used in planners and journals, flag stickers can also be used for other purposes, such as marking important pages in a book or labeling items in a file folder.

Planner sticker shops that sell sticker sets will often include a sheet of flag stickers in their packs. Or they may combine a sheet of stickers with half being flag stickers and the other half being dot stickers.

Functional Stickers: Functional write-on stickers are a type of planner sticker that is designed to be written on with a pen or marker. They are typically made from a special type of paper or material that is compatible with writing instruments and can be easily written on and erased without smudging or bleeding.

Functional write-on stickers are often used in planners and journals to mark tasks or events that need to be completed. They can be used in place of traditional stickers or in conjunction with them to provide a more flexible way to note dates. Functional write-on stickers can come in a variety of shapes, sizes, and colors to suit different planning needs and styles. They can be used to mark daily, weekly, and monthly tasks or events, as well as special occasions and holidays.

There are a few types of sticker paper that you can use to print stickers that you can write on. One option is clear or transparent sticker paper, which allows you to print your sticker design and then write on the sticker with a pen or marker. Another option is white matte sticker paper, which is a non-glossy paper that you can print your design on and then write on with a pen or marker. Both of these types of sticker paper are widely available at office supply stores, craft stores, and online.

Quote Stickers: Quote stickers are a type of planner sticker that feature quotes or phrases that are usually intended to inspire or motivate the user, although they can also be sarcastic in an attempt at humor. These types of stickers can be used in planners and journals as a way to add a personal touch and provide a bit of inspiration or a laugh as the user works through their tasks. They can also be used to decorate the outside of planners, notebooks, and journals.

Both planner and individual Etsy sticker shops may offer a variety of quote stickers to suit different customers. These can include daily, weekly, and monthly quote stickers, as well as stickers for special occasions and holidays. They can also include a variety of colors, sizes, and shapes to suit different preferences.

Note that most Etsy sticker shops offer quote stickers in their own sets or as individual sheets. You can typically charge more for quote stickers as they are larger and more niche than traditional sheets of planner stickers. However, if you are selling planner stickers, you want to make sure any quote stickers you design have the same aesthetic. For example, you don't want to offer Bible verse stickers next to curse word stickers.

Sidebar Stickers: Planner sidebar stickers are a type of planner sticker that is designed to be used in the sidebar edge of a planner or journal. The sidebar is a section of the planner that is typically located on the right or left side of the page and is used to mark specific tasks or events, or simply to jot down notes.

Etsy planner sticker shops may offer a variety of sidebar stickers to suit different planning needs and styles. These can include daily, weekly, and monthly sidebar stickers, as well as stickers for special occasions and holidays. They can also include a variety of colors, sizes, and shapes to suit different preferences. In addition to being used in planners and journals, sidebar stickers can also be used for other purposes, such as marking important pages in a book or labeling items in a file folder.

Sidebar stickers are a common part of planner sticker sets. Some planner users want the ability to write on sidebar stickers, so make note of that if you plan to offer them in your shop as you'll need to have them printed on non-glossy, matte sticker paper.

So, what are the best products to offer in an Etsy planner sticker shop? Do you need to offer every type of sticker mentioned above?

Your first decision will be whether you want to offer stickers that users can write on as this will require you to use sticker paper that is non-glossy and matte. Most traditional planner sticker shops do offer stickers that can be written on. However, if you do not want to offer those types of stickers, you don't have to. Instead, you can focus on creating stickers for special occasions and holidays as well as decorative stickers.

Most planner sticker shops start with one type of sticker and add it to their offerings as they learn what customers like. Perhaps they started with decorative stickers but then grew to offer personalized stickers. And, as they grow, sticker shop owners may also expand from just planner stickers to other planner and stationery accessories such as pens, notepads, journals, pins, mousepads, and even bags. The opportunities are endless...if you want to grow. However, it's also okay to JUST focus on selling stickers.

You may be asking why buyers would come to Etsy for planner stickers when there are so many already on the market. Every craft and big box store has aisles filled with planner stickers, plus there are many planner companies that sell online including Erin Condren, Happy Planner, and Cloth & Paper.

The reason shoppers turn to Etsy for planner stickers is that they are looking for something that big-name brands can't offer. Successful Etsy sticker shops are providing consumers with stickers they can't find anyplace else. Before you launch your own Etsy planner sticker shop, take time to look in the stores and online to see what brands are already offering. Note what you see a lot of. Then think of themes and designs that they aren't offering for sale and focus on those. You'll never be able to compete with the major brands by selling items similar to theirs; instead, focus on what isn't for sale.

If you are wanting to start a planner sticker shop, chances are it is because you use planners and had the idea to create stickers for your own use, now realizing you could turn your passion into a business. What stickers are you not able to find in stores? Ask your friends and family if they use planners and, if so, what stickers they would like to see on the market. As with any good business model, you'll want to "think outside the box" when it comes to designing stickers and finding success with an Etsy planner sticker shop!

Vinyl Sticker Shops: While planner sticker shops are the most popular type of Etsy sticker shop, in second place are vinyl sticker shops. But what exactly are vinyl stickers?

When I started my own Etsy sticker shop, I knew I wanted to create single stickers, not planner stickers or even sticker sheets. I like individual, larger stickers that I can collect or use on notebook covers. I had ideas for stickers in mind before I even knew how I would produce them. However, I didn't realize that Etsy customers weren't shopping for just any stickers, they were buying VINYL stickers.

Why vinyl stickers? Vinyl stickers are waterproof, heat-safe, and scratch resistant. Buyers purchase vinyl stickers to put on their water bottles and laptops. That's why vinyl stickers are almost always also referred to as "waterproof stickers." Vinyl waterproof stickers are safe for the dishwasher and can handle spills. Besides water bottles and laptops, they are also popular for decorating the covers of planners, journals, and notebooks; and they are even safe to put on cars.

While you can print and cut vinyl stickers using the same equipment as you would for planner stickers and sheet sets, most Etsy sticker shops that sell vinyl stickers outsource their printing of them. I will discuss this further in Chapter Five, but for now, I will tell you that I and many sticker shop owners order our vinyl stickers from a company called StickerMule. I simply upload my designs to their website and they print, cut, and ship the stickers to me. I then list them in my Etsy shop and ship them whenever an order comes in.

As with planner sticker shops, sometimes single sticker shops expand into other products such as sticker sheets and other stationery items. They may even start to offer planner stickers. StickerMule, along with some other sticker printers, does offer sticker sheets, making it easy to create sheets of smaller stickers using your most popular single sticker designs. And you can even offer print-on-demand sticker sheets through companies such as Printify and Printful.

Regardless of if you plan to sell single stickers or expand into sheets, as with planner stickers, single sticker shops must have a cohesive look and stick to a general theme. After all, you are building a brand. You want to have enough products to appeal to as many buyers as possible, but you don't want to confuse potential customers by having designs that are all over the place. For instance, you don't want to list religious-themed stickers alongside stickers with adult themes. With any Etsy shop, you want customers to stay in your shop, buy multiple items, and then return later to purchase more.

The good news is that you can have multiple Etsy sticker shops under one account. If you decide you want to offer drastically different themes and designs, you can simply open a second or even third shop.

Keep in mind that you will need to have a separate email address for your new shop, as Etsy does not allow multiple shops to be linked to the same email. Note that Etsy sometimes automatically shuts down new shops before you even list one item. This is due to their use of bots reviewing information and seeing that you already have a store. Simply message Etsy directly to let them know that you are setting up a second shop. They will confirm your information and make your new shop active for you.

Other Types of Sticker Shops: While planner stickers and single vinyl stickers are the two most popular types of Etsy sticker shops, there are some other options for selling stickers, including one that doesn't require you to print or ship stickers yourself!

Sheets of Stickers: As we've discussed, planner stickers aren't the only kind of stickers that are printed on sheets. Sheets of stickers that people can use for any purpose are also popular. Perhaps you have a cute design of a panda. You can have it printed in single sticker form or you could create a sticker sheet with the design duplicated in multiple smaller sizes. If you aren't printing and cutting your stickers, a company such as StickerMule can produce sticker sheets for you.

Printable Stickers: If you love the design element of creating sticker sheets but don't want the expense of printing, cutting, and shipping them, you can sell your stickers as downloadable files that customers print themselves. Once you've created a page of stickers on your computer, you would skip the printing part and instead upload the file straight to Etsy. Customers would then purchase the file, download it onto their computer, and print the stickers out using their printer onto their sticker paper. They would then need to use their cutting machine to complete the process.

Sticker Templates: Selling sticker templates is similar to selling printable stickers, except, in this instance, you would leave room for the buyer to customize the stickers themselves. Perhaps you create a sheet of name tag stickers, for instance. You provide the layout along with all colors and design elements. The buyer would then manually enter names on their end and finish printing. Companies such as Avery offer a wide range of peel-and-stick badges and labels. By matching their measurements to your templates, customers wouldn't need to cut the stickers. Instead, they would simply purchase the ready-made labels, which are available at office supply stores, big box stores, and Amazon.

Custom Stickers: Custom stickers go somewhat hand-and-hand with sticker templates. Let's think about the example I just used about selling templates for name tags. In the case of selling custom stickers, the buyer would provide you with the names they wanted to be added to the tags. You would then be able to either provide them with the completed file for them to print; or if you have printing capabilities, you will also print and ship them their labels.

TO RECAP: While planner stickers and single vinyl stickers are the most common sticker shops on Etsy, there is seemingly no limit to the types of stickers you can offer in your shop. Whether you want to only offer one type of sticker or grow your shop to offer multiple products, the only thing that stands in your way is your desire and imagination!

CHAPTER FOUR: HOW TO DESIGN STICKERS

Before you can sell stickers on Etsy, you first need to create stickers! As we've already discussed in previous chapters, there are two main types of Etsy sticker shops: planner sticker shops and vinyl sticker shops. Sometimes shops carry both and sometimes shops carry additional products. But the first order of business for any sticker shop is designing the stickers themselves.

First in the sticker creation process is the actual design of the sticker. There are several ways you can design stickers:

- Hand-draw the stickers yourself
- Use graphic design software to create stickers
- Purchase print-on-demand graphics licensed from designers
- Hire a graphic designer to create your sticker designs
- A combination of two or more of the above

Hand-drawing stickers: When we talk about hand-drawing stickers, we are referring to drawing sticker designs using a tablet or computer, not pen and paper. The three most popular tools used to draw stickers are:

1. **iPad (Pro or Air)**
2. **Apple Pencil**
3. **Procreate**

iPad & Apple Pencil: Many sticker designers use an iPad and an Apple Pencil because these tools offer several advantages for creating digital artwork. Some of the reasons why an iPad and an Apple Pencil may be preferred by sticker designers include:

- **Portability:** An iPad and Apple Pencil are portable, making it easy to create digital art on the go.
- **Ease of use:** The iPad and Apple Pencil are intuitive and easy to use, making it quick and easy to create digital art.
- **Precision:** The Apple Pencil is highly precise and responsive, making it ideal for creating detailed and accurate artwork.
- **Wide range of features:** The iPad and Apple Pencil offer a wide range of features and tools for creating digital art, such as layers, blending modes, and customizable brushes.
- **Compatibility with other software:** The iPad and Apple Pencil are compatible with a wide range of digital art software, including Procreate and Adobe Illustrator, making it easy to create and edit digital art.

Procreate: Procreate is a popular digital drawing and illustration app for the iPad and iPhone. It is designed for artists and creative professionals who want to create digital art using a wide range of tools and features. And it is overwhelmingly the choice most Etsy sticker shop designers use to create their products.

Procreate includes a variety of features that make it easy to create high-quality digital art, including a customizable interface, a wide range of brushes, layers, and blending modes, and support for high-resolution canvases. It also includes tools for drawing, painting, sketching, and lettering, as well as features for exporting and sharing finished artwork. And since it works seamlessly with an iPad and Apple Pencil, it is the perfect software for creating stickers.

While Procreate is the most popular design app for creating stickers when using an iPad, there are other programs you can use to create stickers, including:

Affinity Designer: Affinity Designer is a vector graphics software that is designed for creating professional-grade designs for print and digital media and can be a great alternative to Procreate for designing stickers. It is available for Mac, Windows, and iPad, and is known for its powerful features and intuitive interface.

ArtRage: ArtRage is a digital painting and drawing software that is designed to replicate the experience of using traditional art media such as oil paints, watercolors, and pastels. It is available for Mac, Windows, and iOS devices and is known for its realistic rendering of traditional art media and its intuitive interface.

Artstudio Pro: While ArtRage and Artstudio Pro are both digital painting and drawing software, there are a few key differences. Artstudio Pro is only available on Mac and Windows. And Artstudio Pro also has a customizable interface, and it offers a wider range of features and tools, including support for vector graphics and more sophisticated import and export options.

Assembly: Assembly is a graphic design and prototyping app for iOS devices such as the iPad. It is designed to make it easy for users to create and prototype designs for digital media. It includes a variety of tools and features that make it easy to create sticker designs with a wide range of customizable shapes and text.

Autodesk SketchBook: Autodesk Sketchbook is a digital drawing and painting software that is designed for creating professional-grade digital art. It is available for Mac, Windows, iOS, and Android devices and is known for its wide range of tools and features, high-quality output, and intuitive interface.

Clip Studio Paint: Clip Studio Paint is a digital drawing and painting software that is designed for creating professional-grade digital art. It is available for Mac, Windows, and iOS devices and is known for its wide range of tools and features, high-quality output, and customizable interface.

Concepts: Concepts is a digital drawing and design app that is available for iOS, Android, and Windows devices. It is designed to make it easy for users to create and sketch out ideas, designs, and other visual concepts using a variety of tools and features.

Drawing Desk: Powered by Cort3ex, Drawing Desk is a digital drawing and painting app that is available for iOS and Android devices. It is designed to make it easy for users to create digital art using a wide range of tools and features. It is popular among artists, illustrators, and other creative professionals who want to create digital art using a mobile device.

Infinite Painter: Infinite Painter is a digital drawing and painting app that is available for Android and iOS devices. It is designed to make it easy for users to create digital art using a wide range of tools and features. Infinite Painter includes a variety of tools and features that make it easy to create digital art, such as a wide range of customizable brushes and pens, support for layers and blending modes, and a range of customization options.

MediBang Paint: MediBang Paint is a digital drawing and painting software that is available for Mac, Windows, iOS, and Android devices. It is designed to make it easy for users to create digital art using a wide range of tools and features. MediBang Paint includes a variety of tools and features that make it easy to create digital art, such as a wide range of customizable brushes and pens, support for layers and blending modes, and a range of customization options. It is popular among artists, illustrators, and other creative professionals who want to create digital art using a mobile device or desktop computer.

Many of the apps listed have a free option to test out. I would suggest downloading all of them that are compatible with your system and trying each one to see which you like best.

But wait. **What if you aren't an artist?** What if you just love stickers and want to open a sticker shop but do not draw your stickers?

No fear, as hand-drawing stickers are just one option for designing stickers for your shop. Other methods don't require you to even touch an Apple Pencil!

Graphic Design Software: Many of the apps we've already discussed allow you to create sticker designs by combining elements and graphics within the app. But if you don't have a tablet, there are just as many desktop software options for creating designs by combining elements such as shapes, colors, and text that are offered within the programs.

The two most popular graphic design software options are:

- **Adobe Illustrator**
- **Adobe Photoshop**

Adobe Illustrator and Adobe Photoshop are both professional graphic design software programs, but they have some key differences:

Similarities:

- Both programs are part of the Adobe Creative Suite and are designed for creating and editing digital graphics.
- Both programs also have a wide range of features and tools for manipulating images and creating professional-quality designs.

Differences:

- Illustrator is a vector graphics editor, which means that it is designed for creating scalable graphics that can be resized without loss of quality. Photoshop is a raster graphics editor, which means that it is designed for editing and manipulating pixel-based images.

- Illustrator is better suited for creating logos, graphics, and illustrations, while Photoshop is better suited for editing and retouching photographs.
- Illustrator has more advanced tools for creating and editing vector shapes and paths, while Photoshop has more advanced tools for adjusting and manipulating the color, lighting, and texture of images.

Both Adobe Illustrator and Adobe Photoshop are capable of creating designs for stickers, but they are suited to different types of stickers. If you want to create a sticker that is a simple shape or text, with solid colors and no intricate details, Illustrator may be the better choice. Illustrator's vector-based tools are well-suited to creating simple, clean designs that can be scaled to any size without loss of quality.

If you want to create a sticker that has a photograph or a more detailed, complex design, Photoshop may be the better choice. Photoshop's raster-based tools are well-suited to editing and manipulating pixel-based images, and it has a wide range of features for adjusting color, lighting, and texture.

Ultimately, the best program for designing stickers will depend on your specific needs and the type of stickers you want to create. If you are just starting and are not sure which program to use, you may want to try experimenting with both Illustrator and Photoshop to see which one you prefer. And while there are no free trials for either Adobe Illustrator or Adobe Photoshop, both are available as part of a Creative Cloud subscription, which allows you to access and use the latest versions of these programs and other Adobe creative tools.

Creative Cloud subscriptions are available with different pricing plans and options to suit different needs and budgets. Some options include:

- A single app subscription, which gives you access to a single Adobe app, such as Illustrator or Photoshop, for a monthly fee.
- A Creative Cloud All Apps subscription, which gives you access to all of the Adobe Creative Cloud apps, including Illustrator and Photoshop, for a monthly fee.
- A free Creative Cloud trial, which allows you to try out the Creative Cloud apps, including Illustrator and Photoshop, for a limited time before deciding whether to purchase a subscription.

If you are a student or teacher, you may be eligible for discounted Creative Cloud subscriptions through Adobe's education pricing program. There are also several free, open-source alternatives to Illustrator and Photoshop that you may want to consider, such as Inkscape and GIMP. These programs may not have all the features and tools of the Adobe Creative Cloud apps, but they can be a good option for basic graphic design tasks. And they can allow you to test out designing your stickers before committing to the purchase of the software at full price.

Canva: Canva is a graphic design software that allows users to create a wide range of visual content, including social media posts, logos, presentations, posters, and more. It is available as a web-based application and as a mobile app for iOS and Android devices.

One of the main features of Canva is its extensive library of templates, which allows users to create professional quality designs quickly and easily. It also has a wide range of design tools and features, including a drag-and-drop interface, pre-designed elements and graphics, and the ability to upload and use your images and fonts.

Canva is designed to be user-friendly and accessible to users with little to no design experience, making it a popular choice for individuals and businesses looking to create visual content for social media, marketing, and other purposes. It is available as a free, ad-supported service, or as a paid subscription with additional features and capabilities.

I use Canva for not only my Etsy sticker shop but also for creating tee shirt designs for Merch by Amazon, Etsy Print-On-Demand, book covers, and social media needs. Whether I'm creating a Facebook banner, an Instagram ad, or changing the colors of a graphic for a sticker, Canva is the only website I use.

Canva has a basic free version, which is great if you want to test it out; but if you are serious about using it for an Etsy sticker shop, I recommend upgrading to the Pro Version, which is $12.95 per month ($9.95 a month if you pay for the year upfront). Not only does Canva Pro provide you with more options, but you can also use the graphics and photos they provide in your print-on-demand items, including stickers. And while I don't recommend using a Canva Pro graphic unedited as a sticker design, as many other people will likely have already done so, I use their graphics as elements in my designs.

Canva also allows you to change the color of graphics, which I often do. For instance, I might have a purchase a graphic for a sticker that is light blue; but with Canva, I can change the shade of blue or even make it a completely different color.

Another way I use Canva to create stickers is to add text to graphics. Canva offers hundreds of fonts and elements that you can experiment with in terms of size, position, and color.

Canva is a useful tool for creating attractive thumbnail photos for my Etsy listings. To do this, I use a background on Canva that looks like a wood wall and place my sticker graphics on top of it. Once I'm happy with the design, I save it as a PNG and then upload it to my Etsy listing from my hard drive when I create a new listing. This makes it easy to create professional-looking photos for my Etsy shop as well as giving it a cohesive look.

Purchase Graphics: While some Etsy shop owners create their original art for their sticker shops, others choose to purchase artwork from artists and graphic designers to use in their products. This is a common practice, particularly for shops that sell individual stickers rather than planner stickers. In fact, the majority of my sticker designs are purchased from other artists and graphic designers.

So how do you go about finding and purchasing graphics for your sticker shop?

There are many websites where you can purchase graphics that come with a print-on-demand license, which allows you to use the graphics on products that you intend to sell, such as tee shirts, book covers, and stickers. This is different from a standard commercial license, which is used for using graphics in advertising. When you buy an image for print-on-demand use, you are purchasing the right to use that image on a product that you will sell.

Note that it is important to be aware of the licensing terms for the graphics you purchase, as different websites may have different policies. Some websites offer a print-on-demand license on all their graphics, while others may charge extra for the use of certain images on products that will be sold. When using Canva Pro, for instance, all their images are cleared for print-on-demand use. However, on Creative Fabrica, you must choose the print-on-demand filter to find images that you can put on items you intend to sell.

Here are some of the most popular websites that offer images you can use to create and sell stickers:

CreativeFabrica.com: Creative Fabrica is a well-known website for purchasing images, fonts, and other design resources. It offers a large selection of resources from various designers, including graphics that can be used for stickers, book covers, and book interiors, as well as a wide range of fonts. The website has over one million design resources and is constantly adding more.

There are several advantages to using Creative Fabrica for purchasing design resources to create stickers. One of the main benefits is the sheer size of the website and the wide range of products available. With over one million design resources, you are likely to find something that meets your needs. Additionally, the website is easy to use and offers relatively affordable prices, making it a convenient and cost-effective option for finding design resources.

One potential disadvantage of using Creative Fabrica is that, because it is such a popular website, it may be harder to find unique designs that haven't already been used by many other people. This is particularly true if you are looking for more specific or detailed graphics, as these are more likely to have been used by multiple people. As a result, it may be harder to find original and unique designs for your sticker shop on Creative Fabrica.

That being said, Creative Fabrica does have a large selection of graphics and fonts to choose from, so it may still be a good option for finding resources for your sticker shop. You may just need to spend a little more time searching and be prepared to look at a larger number of options to find something that meets your needs.

PRO TIP: To help find unique and original graphics on Creative Fabrica for your sticker shop, try changing the search filter to "newest first" when searching for graphics on the site. This will show you the newest images that have been added to the site, which may be less likely to have been used by other sellers. With so many sticker shops using Creative Fabrica for images, it's important to take steps to ensure that you aren't using designs that are already in use by other sellers.

Changing the search filter to "newest first" can help you find fresh and original graphics for your shop.

It's important to note that just because someone else has already used a graphic from Creative Fabrica for a sticker doesn't necessarily mean that you can't use it as well. Depending on the licensing terms for the graphic, you may still be able to use it for your stickers, as long as you are using it following the terms of the license.

However, if you do find a graphic on Creative Fabrica that you like but that has already been used by another seller, you may want to consider using a tool like Canva to alter the coloring or add text to the image to make it more unique and original. This can help you create a design that is more distinctive and stands out from other stickers that may be using the same or similar graphics.

As I mentioned earlier in this chapter, the licensing terms for the graphics on Creative Fabrica may vary depending on the specific image. Some images may be available for purchase under a "commercial" license, while others may be available under a "print-on-demand" license. It is important to carefully review the licensing terms for any graphic that you are considering using to ensure that you are using it following the terms of the license.

If you are using the graphic for a sticker that you intend to sell, you need to make sure that you are using a graphic that is available under a "print-on-demand" license. This type of license gives you the right to use the graphics on products that you intend to sell, such as stickers. A "commercial" license, on the other hand, may only give you the right to use the graphics for advertising or on a website, and may not allow you to use them on products that you plan to sell.

Creative Fabric offers a "print-on-demand" license filter on the left-hand side of their search page. Make sure you select this option anytime you are searching for images to use for stickers or any other products you intend to sell.

Creative Fabrica offers a variety of options for purchasing design resources, including both monthly subscriptions and individual graphics. Note that they frequently offer specials on their subscription packages. My advice is to sign up for a free account with them and then wait for an email offer or browse the site and wait for a pop-up deal. I've currently extended my Creative Fabrica subscription for two years as they offered me such a great deal.

DepositPhotos: DepositPhotos is a website that offers high-quality images for purchase, but the prices can be quite expensive and the licensing terms for using the images on products that you intend to sell can be complex. While DepositPhotos does offer an Extended License for print-on-demand use, the cost for this license can be close to $100 for a single image, which may not be feasible for many people.

Despite the high prices and complex licensing terms, I have found DepositPhotos to be a useful source of inspiration for sticker designs. I have also noticed that some of the images available on DepositPhotos can be found on other websites for less expensive prices. This is because many of the images on DepositPhotos are from individual designers who may also sell their work on other websites.

While I may not personally use DepositPhotos for my sticker designs due to the high prices and complex licensing terms, I do think it can be a useful source of images for social media and advertising. DepositPhotos often has big sales around the holidays where you can purchase graphics packages at a discount, which can be a good opportunity to stock up on images for these purposes.

Dreamstime: Like DepositPhotos, Dreamstime is a website that offers a wide range of high-quality images and illustrations that can be used for creating stickers. However, similar to DepositPhotos, the licensing terms for using the images on products that you intend to sell can be complex and may vary depending on the specific image. Some images may be available for free and include a print-on-demand license, while others may be quite expensive and only include a limited license. This can make it difficult to understand exactly what you are allowed to do with the images that you purchase from Dreamstime.

Despite the potential challenges with the licensing terms, I have found Dreamstime to be a useful source of inspiration for sticker designs. The website has a large selection of images and illustrations to browse, and you can often find some useful royalty-free images for use in your advertising and social media. While it may not be the best option for purchasing graphics for your sticker designs, it can be a good resource to consider when looking for inspiration or other types of design resources.

Etsy: Etsy isn't just the best website for running a sticker shop, it can also be a good place to purchase images and design elements to use in creating stickers. The advantage of buying graphics on Etsy is that you can often find unique and original designs that may not be available on other websites. Many of the graphics on Etsy are created by independent designers and artists, so you may be able to find some truly one-of-a-kind designs.

The downside to buying sticker images on Etsy is that other sticker shops may have already purchased the same images for their designs. Therefore, be sure to buy newly listed graphics that others haven't bought and use a site like Canva to slightly alter the images. As always, ensure any image you buy on Etsy comes with a print-on-demand license that allows you to print and sell the image on stickers and other products.

PicMaker: If you have photos that you would like to use as the basis for your sticker designs, PicMaker.com may be a good option to consider. This website offers a range of tools and features for creating and editing images, including the ability to add your photos and a selection of over 100 million stock images that you can use to enhance your designs.

PicMaker offers a free option if you would like to try out the site and see what it has to offer. If you decide to sign up for a paid plan, prices start at $7.99 per month.

Shutterstock: Shutterstock is a website that offers a large library of high-quality images, music, and videos, with new products being added regularly. In addition to its extensive selection of media, Shutterstock also includes a built-in image editor that you can use to modify and customize images to your liking.

The advantage of using Shutterstock for creating stickers is that you have access to a vast collection of professional-quality media that you can use in your designs. Additionally, the built-in image editor can be a useful tool for making small adjustments to the images you use in your designs, such as cropping or resizing.

The biggest downside of using Shutterstock is the cost, with packages starting at $29 per month for a limited number of images. For example, at the $29 per month level, you are only allowed to download 10 images per month. To access a higher number of images, you will need to purchase a more expensive package, such as the $169 per month plan, which allows you to download 350 images per month.

StickerMule: I use StickerMule for printing my stickers, but they also have a design section on their website where you can create custom stickers using pre-loaded templates. These templates include options for circle, square, and oval stickers, as well as bumper stickers. The templates are easy to use, and once you have designed your sticker, you can place an order right on the site.

It's worth noting that the template options on StickerMule's design section are somewhat limited and aren't as elaborate or creative as other sites offer. However, these templates can still be a useful resource for experimenting with basic design if you are new to this type of work and can be a good way to create simple quote stickers or other basic designs. Even if you have more advanced design skills, the templates on StickerMule's website may still be a convenient and efficient way to create basic stickers quickly and easily.

Hire a Graphic Designer to Create Your Stickers: If you are finding it difficult to navigate the various websites and options for finding graphics for your stickers, or if the thought of selecting images or editing your photos feels too daunting, there is another option to consider: hiring someone to design your stickers for you.

Hiring a graphic designer to create stickers for you is a good solution if you don't have the time, skills, or resources to create your own graphics, or if you want to get more professional-quality results than some of the traditional graphics sites offer. Many talented graphic designers are available for hire, either on a freelance basis or through a design agency. These designers can create custom graphics for your stickers, using your ideas and specifications as a starting point. By working with a professional designer, you can get the high-quality results you want without having to worry about the technical aspects of design.

There are many websites, such as Fiverr and UpWork, that offer a wide range of design and creative services, including artists who will design stickers for you. Fiverr is often considered to be the most affordable option for hiring a graphic designer, with prices starting at as low as $5 for some types of services. This can be a good way to get professional-quality results at a lower cost, especially if you are working on a tight budget. However, it's important to keep in mind that the quality of work may vary depending on the individual designer you choose, and you may need to spend more to get the level of quality you want.

On Fiverr, for example, you can search for keywords like "create stickers" or "sticker design" to find designers who offer these types of services. The search results will typically include a range of designers with different skills and experience levels, along with details about their services and pricing.

When hiring a designer on a platform like Fiverr, you will typically start by describing your project and sharing your ideas or concepts with the designer. The designer will then work with you to develop the design and create the graphics files that you need. It's important to keep in mind that the designer will not be responsible for producing the physical stickers - they will only create the graphic file that you can then use to have the stickers printed.

UpWork designers typically charge more for their services than those on Fiverr. However, the quality of work reflects the price. It is possible to connect with a designer on UpWork and develop a working relationship where they create several sticker designs for you. You can post a job notice on UpWork with details on what you are looking for and a starting budget. Designers will then submit proposals to you for you to review.

In addition to Fiverr and UpWork, you can also find freelance sticker designers on the following websites:

99designs: This platform is specifically focused on design services, including graphic design, logo design, and branding. You can browse through portfolios of designers and choose the one that best meets your needs.

PeoplePerHour: This platform offers a wide range of services, including design and creative work. You can search for designers and other freelancers based on your specific needs and get quotes for the work you want to be done.

Freelancer: This is a large platform that connects clients with freelancers and independent contractors in a wide range of fields, including design and creative work. You can post your project and receive proposals from interested freelancers.

Guru: This platform offers a range of design and creative services, including graphics for stickers. You can search for and hire designers based on their skills and experience.

A Combination of Two or More Methods: Many Etsy sticker shop owners use a combination of different methods to create their designs. Some may hand-draw their stickers and then use graphic design software to make final adjustments, while others may purchase graphics from a site like Creative Fabrica and then customize them using a tool like Canva. Some shop owners may also hire designers through platforms like Fiverr or UpWork to create custom graphics and then incorporate elements from other sources as well. There is no one "right" way to create sticker designs, and shop owners often use a combination of different techniques to create unique and attractive products.

How I Create My Stickers: Although I am not an artist, I like to create stickers by purchasing a print-on-demand license for graphics that have been designed by professional artists. I often use a tool like Canva to customize these images by changing their colors, adding text, or removing elements. This allows me to create unique stickers that reflect my style and vision, even if I don't have the artistic skills to build the designs from scratch. I find that this method works well for me, and I'm able to produce high-quality stickers that I can be proud to sell in my Etsy shop.

In addition to purchasing graphics from professional designers, I also create some of my sticker designs using Canva alone. This includes text-based stickers that consist of words with no accompanying images. Canva offers a wide variety of fonts and other design elements, such as photos, images, and vectors, which I can use to create custom stickers that reflect my style and brand. With a Pro License, I have access to even more resources that can help me bring my sticker ideas to life.

After creating a design for a sticker, the next step is to print the actual physical stickers. There are several options for printing stickers, each with its pros and cons. Here are a few options to consider:

- Print the stickers yourself using a home printer and sticker paper
- Use a professional printing service
- Use a print-on-demand service

Not sure which is the method for you? The next chapter will go into more detail about the different options for printing stickers to sell in your own Etsy sticker shop!

CHAPTER FIVE: HOW TO PRODUCE PHYSICAL STICKERS TO SELL

You now know how to design stickers. But to sell stickers on Etsy, you need to have actual stickers to list and ship. So how do you produce physical stickers to sell?

There are three ways to manufacture stickers for an Etsy sticker shop:

- **Print the stickers yourself using a home printer and sticker paper:** This is an affordable option, but it can be time-consuming and may not produce the highest-quality results.
- **Use a professional printing service:** Many online printing services specialize in printing stickers. These services typically offer a range of materials, sizes, and quantities to choose from, and can produce high-quality stickers quickly and efficiently. However, they can be more expensive than printing the stickers yourself.
- **Use a print-on-demand service:** There are also print-on-demand services that will produce and ship stickers to your customers as orders come in. This eliminates the need for you to keep an inventory of stickers, but it can also be more expensive than other options.

My sticker shop mainly features single, vinyl stickers. As I've previously mentioned, I use a company called StickerMule to print my stickers. I simply upload my design files to their website and choose the type of sticker I want, such as die-cut, clear, circle, or holographic. Later in this chapter, I will provide a list of other sticker printers that you may want to consider if, like me, you want to outsource your sticker printing.

However, before discussing those options, I will first go over the process of printing stickers yourself using a home printer and sticker paper.

PRINTING YOUR OWN STICKERS: Many planner sticker shops choose to print their stickers in-house using a color printer and a cutting machine, such as a Cricut. This allows them to produce high-quality stickers quickly and efficiently, without having to rely on a third-party printing service.

By printing and cutting their sticker sheets in-house, these Etsy shop owners can have complete control over the production process and can ensure that their stickers meet their standards of quality. In addition, printing stickers in-house can be a more affordable option over time, if the shop is producing a large volume of stickers and has invested in the best equipment. However, the model of manufacturing stickers does require the initial investment in a good color printer and precise cutting machine, as well as the time and effort to set up and maintain this equipment.

To print your own stickers, you will need the following items:

- **Color Inkjet Printer**
- **Sticker Paper**
- **Cutting Machine**

Color Inkjet Printer: If you choose to print your stickers in-house, the first piece of equipment you will need is a color printer. Many sticker shop owners recommend using an inkjet printer for the best quality. Inkjet printers use liquid ink to produce high-quality images and are generally more versatile than other types of printers, as they can handle a wide range of media, including sticker paper.

Inkjet printers range widely in price, from around $50 to several hundred dollars. When shopping for an inkjet printer, consider factors such as print quality, speed, and cost of ink. Look for a printer that offers good value for the price and has a good reputation for reliability. You may also want to consider purchasing a printer with individual ink cartridges, as this can help save money on ink in the long run.

Here are a few popular inkjet printers that may be worth considering for your sticker business:

1. Canon PIXMA PRO-100: This professional-grade printer is known for its high print quality and wide color range. It is suitable for printing a variety of media, including sticker paper.
2. Epson Expression Photo HD XP-15000: This compact printer is great for small businesses, with a high print resolution and the ability to print borderless photos.
3. HP ENVY Photo 7855: This all-in-one printer is suitable for printing stickers, as well as photos and documents. It offers a range of connectivity options, including mobile printing.
4. Brother MFC-J497DW: This budget-friendly printer is suitable for small businesses and offers a range of features, including automatic duplex printing and mobile connectivity.

Sticker Paper: When it comes to printing stickers, there are two main types of sticker paper to consider: matte and vinyl.

Matte sticker paper is often preferred for planner stickers, as it allows users to write on them easily. On the other hand, vinyl sticker paper is more durable and waterproof, making it ideal for decorative stickers that will be placed on water bottles or other objects that may come into contact with water.

Sticker paper for inkjet printers usually comes in sheets that are 8.5x11 inches in size. Other common sizes include 4x6 inches, 5x7 inches, and 12x12 inches. Some sticker paper is also available in larger sizes, such as 13x19 inches and 11x17 inches. It is important to choose the size of sticker paper that is appropriate for your needs, taking into account the size of the stickers you want to create, the size of your printer, and the ability of your cutting machine to cut various paper sizes. You also want to consider the size of envelopes you will need to ship your stickers, noting that the larger the envelope, the more expensive postage may be.

Cutting Machine: Of course, it's not enough to just print out your stickers. You need to cut the stickers for your customers. And for this task, most sticker shop owners use cutting machines.

Cutting machines, such as Cricut's and Silhouettes, work by using a small blade to precisely cut out shapes or designs from a variety of materials, including sticker paper. The machine is controlled by a computer program that allows the user to input specific shapes or designs, as well as the size and position of the cut. The cutting machine then uses a motor to move the blade along the desired cutting path, following the instructions provided by the program. Some cutting machines also can draw or write using pens or markers.

Additional Supplies: Many sticker shop owners who print their stickers in-house also have other supplies handy, including:

- **Paper Cutter:** For trimming sticker sheets
- **Scissors:** For cutting stickers into individual shapes or designs
- **Ruler:** For measuring and trimming stickers to the desired size
- **Cutting Mat:** For protecting surfaces while cutting stickers
- **Tweezers:** For handling small stickers or for placing stickers onto packaging or planners
- **Sticker Backing:** For attaching to the back of cut stickers to make them easy to peel and stick
- **Sticker Package:** For organizing and storing stickers before

and after they have been cut.

USING A PRINTER COMPANY TO PRINT YOUR STICKERS: If you plan on selling individual vinyl stickers, it's almost always going to be easier, faster, and more cost-effective for you to outsource the printing of your stickers. Numerous online sticker printing companies offer great prices and products; the hard part is choosing the best company for your needs.

But first, how does one go about using an online printer to print stickers?

The process is simple: You create an account with an online printing company and upload your image files to the site. You then choose the size and type of sticker you want the image to be printed on. You will then receive a digital proof to approve. If you are happy with the proof, you can go ahead and complete your order. If you would like to make a change, you can usually request that. Make sure you know if changes are allowed before uploading your file and double-check the proof before committing to an order as most sales are final after you approve your proof.

Some of the top vinyl sticker printing companies currently online include:

StickerMule: Most sticker shop owners, including myself, use StickerMule. StickerMule not only offers good pricing and consistent high-quality stickers, but they also offer a lot of options when it comes to printing your images, including:

Stickers: StickerMule offers the most stickers options, including die-cut, circle, rectangle, square, oval, bumper, sheets, kiss cut, rounded corner, clear, transfer, vinyl lettering, static clings, front adhesive, and holographic. Sizes range from as small as 1" to whatever custom size you want.

Note that most sticker shops carry the die-cut matte stickers, although I have some circle stickers and sticker sheets in my store, along with holographic options that I've gotten from StickerMule. Clear stickers are also a popular choice as the background color of whatever item the sticker is on will show through.

The 3" size is the most popular and widely used size for vinyl stickers, as it allows for flexibility in placement on various surfaces such as water bottles and laptops. On StickerMule, the 3" size is the largest option available before the price significantly increases. This size allows customers to easily create a sticker collage or add multiple stickers to their belongings without running out of space.

Labels: StickerMule offers a wide range of sticker label options to choose from, including rolls and sheets in various shapes and sizes. The available options include clear roll, die cut roll, circle roll, rectangle roll, square roll, oval roll, rounded corner roll, circle sheet, die cut sheet, oval sheet, rectangle sheet, rounded corner, and square sheet. These options allow customers to select the most suitable shape and size for their needs, whether they are looking for individual stickers or sheets of stickers.

Label-style stickers are a great way to promote your brand by printing your logo onto stickers. They can be used as thank-you seals or placed on free gifts to add a professional touch. The sheet label options allow you to print multiple copies of the same sticker, depending on the sheet style you choose. This can be a convenient and cost-effective option if you need to produce a large number of stickers with the same design.

On StickerMule, the "Label Sheet" options tend to be more affordable than the "Sticker Sheet" options. Custom "Sticker Sheets" may cost a few dollars, while "Label Sheets" can start at under $1. It's worth comparing the prices of similar products to ensure that you are getting the best value for your money.

Magnets: Another reason I choose StickerMule for printing my stickers is that they offer items other than stickers, my favorite being magnets. Die-cut vinyl magnets in the same design as your stickers can be a popular addition to your product line and can help to increase your sales. It's a good idea to consider ordering both the sticker and magnet versions when placing a new order and to offer both items in the same listing on Etsy. This can help to give customers more options and encourage them to make a purchase.

Like stickers, magnets are available in a variety of sizes, with 3" being the most common size. Other options include 2", 4", and 5", or you can order custom sizes to meet your specific needs. It's worth noting that magnets tend to be more expensive to produce than stickers, but the price per unit can decrease as you order larger quantities. This is a common pricing strategy among suppliers, including StickerMule.

Buttons: Offering buttons and pins with your designs can be a great way to differentiate your Etsy shop from others and give you an edge over the competition. StickerMule can print your designs onto round, rectangle, and oval buttons, as well as acrylic pins. These items can be a fun and unique way to showcase your designs and attract customers to your shop.

It's important to consider the shipping costs when selling items such as buttons and pins, as they may require a different shipping method than stickers and flat magnets. Stickers and flat magnets can typically be shipped via USPS letter using a stamp, while the thickness of buttons and pins may require them to be shipped via USPS First Class Package, which is more expensive.

Packaging: StickerMule offers custom packaging and shipping supplies such as poly mailers, bubble mailers, and packing tape. While these items can be useful for protecting and shipping your products, they may not be necessary for every order and can be a significant expense. Some people may choose to use these supplies only for special orders or when StickerMule is offering deals on these items. Ultimately, the decision to use these types of supplies will depend on your specific needs and budget.

T-Shirts: If you are looking to sell custom t-shirts with your business logo, there are several options available to you. One option is to use a program such as Merch by Amazon, which allows you to easily create and sell custom t-shirts with no upfront fees. Alternatively, if you only need a small number of t-shirts, you can consider using a service like StickerMule, which offers t-shirts in sizes small to 2XL in a variety of colors. This can be a convenient option if you want to quickly and easily purchase a small number of custom t-shirts.

More Products: Finally, StickerMule offers a variety of products that you can customize with your artwork, including keychains. Keychains can be a popular choice for many designers, but it's worth considering the additional cost of shipping and production when deciding whether to sell them. Some people may choose to use keychains and other similar products more as promotional items or free gifts with large orders, rather than as a primary product to sell. It's a good idea to carefully consider the costs and potential return on investment for these types of products to ensure that they are a viable option for your business.

Acrylic charms, coasters, wall graphics, and floor graphics round out StickerMule's offerings. I feel that StickerMule offers the biggest selection of products at the best price and the best quality for the price.

It's no surprise that most Etsy sticker shops use StickerMule for their individual sticker needs.

One of the main benefits of using StickerMule is the ability to order small sample packs of their most popular products. This can be a great way to test out different designs and materials without committing to a large order and spending a lot of money. In addition, StickerMule offers free shipping on all orders. If you have a state sales tax permit (also called a "reseller's permit), you can upload your certificate to save on the tax.

StickerMule offers the following samples:

- 3" Die-Cut Stickers
- 3" Clear Stickers
- 3" Holographic Stickers
- 3" Magnets
- 3" Custom Label Rolls
- Coasters
- Packing Tape Strip
- Poly Mailers

While other sticker companies also offer sample packs, StickerMule offers the most variety, and most of the sample packs come in quantities of 10. In some cases, purchasing sample packs is more affordable than ordering larger quantities of stickers. For example, a sample pack of 10 die-cut vinyl stickers costs $9, or $0.90 per sticker, while 50 die-cut vinyl stickers cost $60, or $1.20 per sticker. To get the per-sticker price lower than the sample pack price, you would need to order a package of 100 stickers. Sample packs are a good option for businesses that are just starting and want to test the market before committing to large orders of stickers.

StickerMule routinely offers limited-time deals where you can order larger quantities of stickers at a discounted price. These deals can be a great opportunity to save money on your sticker purchases, especially if you are planning to order a large quantity. For example, you may be able to purchase a 50-count pack of holographic stickers for only $29 with free shipping, which is significantly cheaper than the regular price of $80 for 50 stickers. It's worth keeping an eye out for these deals and taking advantage of them when they are available to help save money on your sticker orders.

STICKER NINJA: StickerNinja.com is another website that offers custom sticker printing services and is often the second choice behind StickerMule when it comes to Etsy sticker shop owners looking to order vinyl stickers. Similar to StickerMule, Sticker Ninja allows you to upload your design file and choose from a variety of sticker options, including:

- Die-cut stickers
- Circle stickers
- Rectangle stickers
- Square stickers
- Oval stickers
- Round corner stickers
- Clear stickers
- Holographic stickers
- Removable stickers
- Waterproof stickers
- Glitter stickers

You can also choose from different materials and finishes, such as matte, gloss, and high gloss. Sticker Ninja also offers a range of other products, including buttons, magnets, and t-shirts, which you can customize with your designs. It's worth comparing the options and pricing at both StickerMule and Sticker Ninja to determine which one is the best fit for your needs.

PRINT-ON-DEMAND STICKERS: If you don't want to keep an inventory of stickers on hand, either by printing them yourself or ordering them from an online print shop, you may be interested in using a print-on-demand service that integrates with your Etsy shop. With this option, you can create and sell custom stickers without having to worry about storing and shipping physical products. The print-on-demand service will handle the printing and shipping of the stickers for you.

The two most popular print-on-demand services for stickers are Printful and Printify. These services allow you to create and sell a wide range of custom products, including stickers, without having to manage inventory or handle fulfillment. This can be a convenient option for those who want to focus on the creative side of their business and leave the logistical details to someone else.

In a print-on-demand Etsy sticker shop, customers can purchase custom stickers that are designed by the shop owner and shipped directly to them from a third-party printer. These stickers are typically available in a range of sizes, shapes, and materials, such as vinyl, paper, or clear film.

Most sellers who run print-on-demand businesses of any kind, either on Etsy or on other websites such as Shopify, Amazon, and eBay, utilize Printful or Printify (and sometimes both) for their products. But before we get into the differences between the two, let's first look at how print-on-demand on Etsy works.

When you offer print-on-demand products on Etsy, you need to first create an account with a print provider that is authorized to integrate with Etsy. For example, if you want to sell print-on-demand stickers through Printify, you need to create an account with Printify and link it with your Etsy shop. You would then create your stickers within your Printify account, and the listings would automatically be added to your Etsy shop. Customers then purchase the stickers through your Etsy shop, and when an order is placed, it is automatically sent to Printify for production and fulfillment, meaning Printify prints the stickers and ships them to the customer directly. Sellers then receive a portion of the sales price after all fees and shipping costs are taken out.

Printful.com: Printful is a print-on-demand fulfillment service that enables businesses to sell custom-printed products such as t-shirts, posters, mugs, and other items, including stickers. It works by connecting to an online store or marketplace, such as Shopify or Etsy, and automatically printing and shipping products to customers as orders are placed.

Printful handles all aspects of production, including printing, cutting, and fulfillment, allowing businesses to focus on marketing and sales. They offer a range of customizable product options, including different materials, sizes, and colors, as well as various printing techniques such as screen printing, embroidery, and sublimation.

Printful offers two sticker options:

Kiss Cut Stickers: "Kiss cut" is Printful's term for "die-cut." These stickers are cut into a specific shape or design and are printed as a single sticker. They are made of durable vinyl material and are suitable for indoor or outdoor use, meaning customers can put them on water bottles, laptops, and even their cars.

Kiss-Cut Sticker Sheets: Kiss-cut sticker sheets are sheets of stickers that are printed on a single sheet of vinyl and then cut into individual stickers using a kiss-cut method. The kiss-cut method involves cutting through the vinyl material but stopping just short of cutting through the backing paper, which allows the stickers to be easily peeled off the backing paper. This cutting method works just like a Cricut machine but Printful can print and cut on a much larger scale than someone printing their own stickers.

Kiss-cut sticker sheets can contain multiple stickers of the same design or a variety of different designs, and they are often used for labeling products, packaging, and promotional materials. They can be customized with different sizes, materials, and finishing options, are weather-resistant and can be used both indoors and outdoors. Smaller stickers can also be used in crafting, scrapbooking, and in planners.

Printify.com: Just like Printful, Printify is a print-on-demand fulfillment service that enables businesses to sell custom-printed products such as t-shirts, posters, mugs, and other items, including stickers. It works by connecting to an online store or marketplace, such as Shopify or Etsy, and automatically printing and shipping products to customers as orders are placed.

Printify offers many more options for stickers than Printful, including:

Roll Stickers: These stickers are printed on a roll and are suitable for labeling products or packaging. They are made of durable vinyl material and are suitable for indoor or outdoor use. I use roll stickers as envelope seals.

Sheet Stickers: These stickers are printed on a sheet and, using a similar method to a Cricut machine, are cut out into individual stickers. They are made of paper material and are suitable for indoor use only. These are the types of stickers planner shops offer.

Die-Cut Stickers: These stickers are individually cut into a specific shape or design and are printed as a single sticker. They are made of durable vinyl material and are suitable for indoor or outdoor use. These are the stickers vinyl sticker shops sell to customers who want to put them onto water bottles, laptops, and even cars.

Kiss-Cut Stickers: These stickers are printed on a sheet of vinyl and then cut into individual stickers using the kiss-cut or die-cut method. They are rectangular or square-shaped stickers that can be easily peeled off the backing paper.

Holographic Stickers: These stickers are printed with a holographic effect that gives them a metallic, shimmery appearance. They are made of durable vinyl material and are suitable for indoor or outdoor use. I carry holographic stickers in my Etsy shop, and customers buy them for use on water bottles, laptops, and cars.

Bumper Stickers: Bumper stickers are adhesive labels that are designed to be affixed to the bumper of a car. They are often used to express a person's political or social views, promote a business or product, or simply display a funny or inspirational message. Bumper stickers are typically made of durable, weather-resistant material, such as vinyl, and are designed to withstand the elements and remain in place for an extended period.

Bumper stickers can come in a variety of sizes, shapes, and colors, and can be printed with text, images, or both. They are typically applied to the bumper of a car using a strong adhesive backing but can also be applied to other smooth surfaces such as windows or walls. Some bumper stickers are removable, while others are designed to be permanent.

Note that some Etsy shops only sell bumper stickers. It is a small, niche market and one with little competition.

The Problem With Print-On-Demand: Setting up an Etsy print-on-demand sticker shop certainly sounds like the best of both worlds. You get to create stickers but you don't have to worry about the printing, cutting, or shipping. Plus the cost is much less; you only pay for a subscription to the print provider and then the Etsy listing fees. You don't have to pay for materials, inventory, or shipping supplies. Why doesn't every sticker shop just use a print-on-demand service?

Well, while print-on-demand can be a convenient way to sell stickers on Etsy, it is also more expensive for customers. Because the stickers are printed and shipped individually as orders are placed, the cost of production and fulfillment is higher than if you were to print and ship stickers yourself or even order them in bulk. This can make it very challenging to compete on price with other sellers who can offer lower prices due to their costs being much less.

For example, The cost for a 2" holographic vinyl sticker on Printify is $3.75. In addition, it will cost the customer $4.50 in shipping. That's right: Nearly $5 to ship ONE sticker. If you were shipping that sticker yourself, it would only cost you the price of a stamp.

Compare Printify's sticker cost to that of ordering a sample package of 10 3" vinyl stickers from StickerMule, which comes out to less than $1 each. To ship one sticker to a customer will only cost the price of a stamp. I can build the cost of shipping into the price of my stickers to give customers "free shipping," which helps me stay competitive. I charge customers $4.50 for one 3" sticker, shipping included. That beats charging $8.25 for a 2" sticker using Printify.

So, is using a print-on-demand service just not practical for an Etsy sticker shop? No, there are some scenarios where an Etsy print-on-demand shop model could work. Personalized stickers, oversized stickers, and specialty stickers such as bumper stickers are all good options. But for print-on-demand planner sticker sheets and single vinyl stickers, it's nearly impossible to be competitive on Etsy due to the cost.

The Choice Is Yours: Print your own stickers, order stickers from a printer, or use a print-on-demand service. Each of these shop models has advantages and disadvantages. The great thing about owning your own business is that you get to decide what works best for you. Try a couple of different methods to see which you like and which you don't. And don't be afraid to change things up if you start with one method but later switch to another. After all, you are your own boss and can do as you please with your business!

CHAPTER SIX: HOW TO OPEN YOUR ETSY STICKER SHOP

It is now time to launch your Etsy sticker shop! You should have already determined the type of sticker shop you want to create and have a plan in place for producing your stickers.

The first manner of business is to set up an Etsy seller account. If you have been shopping on Etsy, you already have an account; but you will need to provide additional information to be approved to sell on Etsy, not just buy on the site.

To set up an Etsy seller account, you will need to follow these steps:

1. Go to the Etsy website and click on the "Sell on Etsy" button.
2. Click the "Open your Etsy shop" button.
3. Enter your email address and password to create an account or sign in with an existing account.
4. Choose your shop language, country, and currency.
5. Select a shop name that represents your brand and is memorable to customers.
6. Agree to Etsy's terms of use and policies.
7. Click the "Create your shop" button to complete the process. After setting up your account, you will need to add products and set up payment methods before you can start selling on Etsy.

After you've completed the initial registration, you'll be prompted to **Create Your Etsy Shop** and set up your **Shop Preferences.** Note that you can skip this prompt and go back in later to set up your store.

Note that you can easily set up or edit your policies at any time under the **Settings** link in your **Shop Manager.**

Etsy Shop Preferences are settings that allow you to customize and manage various aspects of your Etsy shop. You can access your shop preferences by going to "Shop Manager" and clicking on the "Preferences" tab.

Here are some of the things you can do in your Etsy Shop Preferences:

- Set your shop location and language.
- Set your shop policies, such as your return policy and shipping policies.
- Customize your shop's appearance by adding a banner image, logo, and other branding elements.
- Set your payment methods and choose which currencies you want to accept.
- Enable automatic renewal for your listings.
- Choose how you want to handle orders, including setting up automatic email responses.
- Set up Google Analytics to track your shop's performance.
- Set up shipping profiles to streamline the process of shipping your products.
- Enable or disable various features, such as the ability to offer gift wrapping or to allow customers to request custom orders.

Time Commitment: Etsy asks about your time commitment as a way to gather information about the sellers on its platform. This information is not used to determine your eligibility to sell on Etsy nor will it affect your shop or seller account in any way. It is simply for informational purposes. You can choose to disclose whether selling on Etsy is your full-time or part-time job, or you can choose not to answer this question. It is entirely up to you.

Shop Name: Your shop name is an important aspect of your branding and should be carefully considered. It's a good idea to choose a shop name that represents your brand and is memorable to customers. It's also a good idea to choose a shop name that is both easy to spell as well as easy to remember.

Keep in mind that you can change your Etsy shop name later on, but it's best to start with a name that you plan to stick with. Changing your shop name can be confusing for your customers and may require you to update your branding materials and marketing efforts, including all your social media accounts and package enclosures.

It's also worth noting that your shop name must adhere to Etsy's naming guidelines and cannot contain any prohibited words or phrases. Etsy has certain requirements and guidelines for shop names to ensure that they are appropriate and do not violate the platform's policies. Here are some of the main requirements and guidelines for shop names on Etsy:

- Shop names must be unique and not already in use by another Etsy seller.
- Shop names must not contain any prohibited words or phrases, such as offensive language or trademarked terms.
- Shop names must not imply that you are affiliated with Etsy or any other company or organization.
- Shop names must not contain any personal information, such as phone numbers or addresses.
- Shop names must not be too long or difficult to spell or pronounce.

- A name that is 4-20 characters in length
- No spaces or special character
- No profanity
- A name not already being used by an existing Etsy member.
- Does not infringe on another's trademark.

I choose my Etsy store name to match the pen name I use to create journals, planners, and coloring books on Amazon. Since stickers fall under "stationery", I thought tying the two together made the most sense and would also cause me less work in the backend part of my businesses, including being able to use my existing Jean Lee Publishing social media pages for my Etsy sticker shop.

My website JeanLeePublishing.com allows visitors to click through to my Amazon books or my Etsy sticker shop. I also have the links to my social media accounts on my website. I run the site through GoDaddy.com, which is also the site I use for all my URLs. My GoDaddy site is basic and inexpensive, but it allows me to link both of my different business sites (Amazon and Etsy) together easily. It also helps bring customers to both my books and my stickers as it is the link I point both Amazon and Etsy shoppers to.

It's important to choose a shop name that is unique and not already in use by another Etsy seller. If the shop name you want to use is already taken, Etsy will provide you with alternative suggestions. However, it's best practice to come up with your original shop name rather than closely copying or mimicking someone else's shop.

Choosing an original shop name can help you stand out on Etsy and establish your own brand identity. As with creating products, you mustn't infringe on anyone else's intellectual property, such as trademarks or copyrights, by using a shop name that is like another seller's name or another brand.

Set Up Payment & Billing: Once you've selected your Etsy shop's name, you'll move on to the next section, which is setting up your payment and billing information. You need to enter a form of payment that Etsy can charge if your fees are greater than your sales. And you need to enter a way for Etsy to pay you.

To set up your Etsy shop's payment and billing, you will need to follow these steps:

1. Go to the "Shop Manager" and click on the "Finances" tab.
2. Click on the "Payment settings" option.
3. Choose your payment method. Etsy allows you to accept payments through PayPal, direct checkout, or both. If you choose PayPal, you will need to enter your PayPal email address. If you choose direct checkout, you will need to enter your credit card information.
4. Set up any additional payment options, such as gift cards or shop credit.
5. Review and accept the terms of use for each payment method.
6. Click the "Save" button to save your payment settings.

The type of information you will need to provide when setting up your Etsy seller account will depend on whether you are registering as an individual/sole proprietorship or as a business. If you do not already have an established business outside of Etsy that is registered as an LLC with the government, you are likely an individual/sole proprietor. In this case, you will need to provide personal information such as your name and contact details. If you are registering as a business, you will need to provide additional information about your business, such as its legal name, contact information, and any relevant documentation.

Confused about the difference between a sole proprietorship and an LLC? Don't worry, most people are. And many people starting businesses are unsure about which is best for their new business.

A **sole proprietorship** is a type of business structure in which an individual owns and operates the business completely by themselves. The owner is responsible for all aspects of the business, including its debts and liabilities. In a sole proprietorship, the owner and the business are considered the same for tax purposes.

On the other hand, a **limited liability company (LLC)** is a business structure that combines elements of both a sole proprietorship and a corporation. Like a sole proprietorship, an LLC is owned by an individual or group of individuals, but it offers its owners the liability protection of a corporation. This means that the owners of an LLC are not personally liable for the debts and obligations of the business.

Both sole proprietorships and LLCs have advantages and disadvantages, and the appropriate choice for your business will depend on your specific needs and circumstances. It is always a good idea to consult with a legal or financial professional before deciding on the best business structure for your company.

Most Etsy sellers, including myself, are sole proprietors. As explained above, being a sole proprietor simply means that I pay taxes as an individual, not a corporation, using my social security number and not a business license.

If you are an individual/sole proprietorship, this means that you are operating your Etsy shop as a one-person business and are not registered as a corporation or LLC with the government. As a sole proprietorship, you will pay taxes (in America) as an individual using your social security number and will not need a business license.

That's right: As a sole proprietor, you do not need to file any type of paperwork with your city, state, or federal governments for your Etsy sticker shop; you will simply be taxed as an individual. Again, this is the case for most places in America; please check with a tax professional or lawyer in your area to see what the requirements are where you live.

The majority of Etsy sellers are individual/sole proprietors, so this is the most common choice if you are starting a sticker shop. If you are registering as an individual/sole proprietorship on Etsy, you will need to provide certain information on the "How you'll get paid" page during the setup process. This information may include:

- Your name and contact information.
- Your social security number or taxpayer identification number (TIN)
- Your bank account information, including the bank name, routing number, and account number.

Credit Card: Because you will be using Etsy's direct checkout to receive payments, you will need to provide your card information on the "How you'll get paid" page during the setup process. It is important to note that you must also provide your bank account information for Etsy to issue payouts to you. In addition, you will need to have a debit or credit card on file with Etsy in case your fees are more than your payouts. In this case, Etsy will charge the balance to your card. It is worth noting that if you sell more than you owe in fees, Etsy will simply deduct the fees from your payouts before issuing them to you.

Test Deposit: After you have entered your payment and billing information on Etsy, the platform may perform a small test deposit to your bank account or PayPal account to verify that the information was entered correctly. This is standard practice to ensure that your deposits are working properly and that you will be able to receive payouts from Etsy.

The test deposit will typically be a small amount, less than a dollar, and you will not be charged for it. To complete the verification process, you will need to check your bank account or PayPal account to find the test deposit and confirm that it was received. Once you have found the test deposit, you can enter the amount on the "How you'll get paid" page to complete the verification process.

It is important to note that the test deposit may take a few days to appear in your account, so be sure to check back periodically if you do not see it right away. If you have any issues with the verification process, you can contact Etsy's support team for assistance. You can easily contact Etsy support at any time and for any reason by following these steps:

1. Go to www.etsy.com and click the "Help & Policies" tab at the bottom of the page.
2. Scroll down to the "Contacting Etsy" section and click the "Contact Us" button.
3. Select the appropriate category for your issue from the dropdown menu.
4. Enter a subject and a detailed description of your issue in the provided fields.
5. Click the "Continue" button to submit your request.

Two-Factor Authentication: Two-factor authentication is an additional security measure that requires you to provide a verification code when signing in from an unrecognized browser or device. This helps to protect your account from unauthorized access and ensures that only you can access your Etsy shop.

To set up two-factor authentication, you will need to choose a method for receiving your verification code. Etsy allows you to receive your verification code in one of three ways:

1. **Text message:** If you choose this option, you will receive a text message with your verification code whenever you need to sign in from an unrecognized browser or device.

2. **Authenticator app:** If you choose this option, you will need to download an authenticator app on your phone and use it to generate

your verification code whenever you need to sign in from an unrecognized browser or device.

3. **Email:** If you choose this option, you will receive an email with your verification code whenever you need to sign in from an unrecognized browser or device.

Set Up Your Storefront: Once you've gotten through entering your personal and banking information, verifying your account, and setting up two-factor authorization, you can move on to a more fun step, which is setting up your Etsy shop storefront!

To set up your Etsy shop storefront, follow these steps:

1. Go to your Etsy seller dashboard and click the "Shop settings" tab.
2. Click the "Shop info & appearance" tab on the left side of the page.
3. Enter a shop title and shop announcement that will appear at the top of your shop's homepage.
4. Add a shop banner image that will appear at the top of your shop's homepage.
5. Add a shop icon, which is a small image that will represent your shop on Etsy.
6. Enter a shop description that will appear on your shop's homepage and in search results.
7. Click the "Save" button to save your changes.

Etsy Shop Title & Shop Announcement: The shop title and shop announcement are elements of your Etsy shop storefront that appear at the top of your shop's homepage. The **shop title** is a short, catchy phrase that represents your shop and its products. The **shop announcement** is a brief message that you can use to communicate important information to your customers, such as new products or promotions.

The shop title and shop announcement are important because they can help to create a first impression on potential customers and set the tone for your shop. You should choose a shop title that accurately reflects the products and style of your shop and craft a shop announcement that is informative and engaging.

Etsy Shop Banner: An Etsy shop banner is a large image that appears at the top of your shop's homepage and gives potential customers an idea of what your shop is all about. The banner image is an important element of your shop's appearance, as it can help to create a professional and cohesive look for your shop and make a good first impression on potential customers.

It is a good idea to choose a banner image that accurately reflects the products and style of your shop, and that is visually appealing and of high quality. You may want to consider hiring a professional graphic designer to create a banner image for you or using a design tool such as Canva to create a banner image on your own. Look at other Etsy shops to see what their banners look like to help you see how to best utilize this design element in your shop.

Note that you can change your banner image at any time.

All Etsy shops can create a shop banner. However, Etsy Plus shop owners, who pay $10 a month for their store subscriptions, have additional banner options:

Carousel Banner: In addition to a standard banner image, Etsy Plus shops can also create a carousel banner on their Etsy shop homepage. A carousel banner is a feature that allows you to add up to four different images that shoppers can scroll through on your shop's homepage. Each image can be linked to a specific listing or shop section, allowing you to showcase your products and direct customers to specific pages within your shop. This feature is great for showcasing new listings as well as featuring holiday items.

To add a carousel banner, simply follow these steps:

1. Go to your Etsy seller dashboard and click the "Shop settings" tab.
2. Click the "Shop info & appearance" tab on the left side of the page.
3. Scroll down to the "Carousel banner" section and click the "Change images" button.
4. Choose up to four images from your computer or use images from your shop's listing photos.
5. For each image, enter a link to a specific listing or shop section in the "Link" field.
6. Click the "Save" button to save your changes.

Collage Banner: A collage banner is a banner image that consists of multiple smaller images arranged together to create a cohesive whole. Collage banners are a popular choice for Etsy Plus shops because they allow you to showcase a variety of products or themes in a single banner image. To create a collage banner for your Etsy shop, you can use a design tool such as Canva or Adobe Photoshop. These tools allow you to combine multiple images into a single banner image and customize the layout and appearance of the banner. Once you have created your collage banner, you can upload it to your Etsy shop as your banner image by following the steps I provided in the "Carousel Banner" section above.

Mixed Grid: All Etsy shops have the option to use a Standard Grid but Etsy Plus shops can also choose a Mixed Grid option that features five listings or shop sections with a couple of layout choices. I like to play around with the various options to see which works best for my shop. And I also periodically change out the images to keep my storefront looking fresh. Top Etsy shops even change out their images daily.

Etsy Shop Icon: Your Etsy shop icon, also referred to as your logo, is a small image that represents your shop on the Etsy platform. It appears next to your shop name on your shop's homepage, on your listings, and on various other pages on the Etsy website and app. Ideally, you want to use this logo across all of your social media, making it the profile picture on all of your platforms.

To set up your Etsy shop icon, you will need to follow these steps:

1. Sign in to your Etsy account and click on the "Shop Manager" button in the top right corner of the page.
2. 2. In the "Shop Settings" section, click on the "Info & Appearance" tab.
3. 3. Scroll down to the "Shop Icon" section and click on the "Change Icon" button.
4. 4. Select the image you want to use as your shop icon from your computer or device. The image must be at least 500 x 500 pixels and in a .jpg, .gif, or .png format.
5. 5. Click on the "Save" button to apply your changes.

Shop Description: An Etsy shop description is a written summary of your shop's products, values, and business philosophy. It is a chance for you to share your brand's story and connect with potential customers on a personal level. A well-written shop description can help to set your shop apart from others on the platform and make it more attractive to potential buyers.

To set up your Etsy shop description, follow these steps:

1. Sign in to your Etsy account and click on the "Shop Manager"

button in the top right corner of the page.

2. In the "Shop Settings" section, click on the "Info &
   Appearance" tab.

3. Scroll down to the "Shop Description" section and click on
   the "Edit" button.

4. In the text editor, write your shop description. Be sure to
   include information about your products, your values, and
   your business philosophy. You can also include any relevant
   details about your process, materials, or inspiration.

5. Click on the "Save" button to apply your changes.

Hiring Out Design Services: You want to use a consistent shop icon
or logo across all of your social media and promotional materials to
create a cohesive brand image. If you can't design your logos and
banners yourself, or you simply don't have the time to create them, you
can hire graphic designers.

There are several places where you can hire a designer to create your
Etsy sticker shop logo, icons, and banners. Some options include:

1. **Fiverr:** Fiverr is an online marketplace where you can find
   freelance designers who offer a wide range of design services,
   including logo and banner design. You can browse through
   portfolios and reviews to find a designer who meets your
   needs and budget.

2. **Upwork:** Upwork is another online marketplace where you
   can find freelance designers for hire. You can post a job listing
   and receive proposals from designers who are interested in
   working with you.

3. **99designs:** 99designs is a design contest platform where you
   can hold a design contest to receive multiple design options
   for your logo, icons, and banners. You can choose the design
   you like best and work with the designer to make any

necessary revisions.

4. **Etsy:** You can also find designers on Etsy who offer design services, including logo and banner design.

Shop Options: You can find **Options** under the **Settings** tab in your shop managers. Etsy allows you to pre-determine several options for your store, including:

Rearrange Your Shop: You can enable the feature to allow shop visitors to sort listings to their specifications. Or you can disable this feature so that the "Most Recently Listed" sort option is chosen.

Custom Order Requests: If you are offering custom or personalized stickers, you can enable a setting where a "Request Custom Order" button will appear across your shop. If you do not offer customized stickers, you will want to disable this feature.

Offer Gift Wrapping: Etsy allows you to enable gift wrapping services in your shop. You can set your own price and the option will appear in every listing. If you do not want to offer gift wrapping, you will want to disable this option.

Offer Gift Message: You can enable or disable the option for buyers to add a message to the packing slip of their order. Believe it or not, people do send stickers as gifts. Since the gift message is automatically included on the packing slip, it is easy to print and include in orders.

Sold Listings: You can choose to let other Etsy users see your sold listings, or you can hide them.

Current Time Zone: You can set your shop's time zone here, which will help Etsy show customers an accurate delivery timeframe.

Vacation Mode: If you ever need to put your Etsy shop on vacation (whether because you are taking an actual vacation or are simply unable to process orders), you can easily put your entire store on vacation so that customers cannot purchase anything from your store. In fact, while your storefront will still be visible, your listings will be hidden. You can also include a Vacation Announcement that will display at the top of your shop. And you can write up a Messages Autoreply, which will be sent to anyone who sends you a message while your Vacation Mode is on.

Close Shop: Also under the Options section is a tab to close your Etsy shop.

Shipping Policies: The shipping settings section of your Etsy account is where you can manage and configure the shipping options for your shop. Note that you can create shipping profiles within each of your listings. When I started my shop, I created a shipping profile when I listed my first product, and can use it across all of my listings.

However, you can create shipping policies within this section if you would like. You can set up shipping profiles, determine shipping costs, and specify shipping destinations. You can also set up automatic shipping rates based on weight, offer free shipping, and set shipping upgrade options.

Note that you can create different shipping profiles for different types of products or destinations and apply the shipping cost accordingly. You can also specify handling time for your products, which means how long it will take for your items to be shipped after an order is placed. This can help buyers to understand when they can expect to receive their orders.

Additionally, you can also choose to offer expedited shipping options and set the prices accordingly. It is important to keep your shipping prices competitive and to take into account any additional costs, such as shipping materials, packaging, and shipping labels.

It is important to keep your shipping profiles updated as shipping rates and regulations can change over time, and you want to make sure that you are providing accurate and fair shipping costs to your customers.

We will cover shipping extensively later on in Chapter Eight of this book.

Policy Settings: Also, under the Settings section is where you can create your Policy Settings. Here you can set up the following:

- **Returns & Exchanges:** Etsy allows sellers to set their own policies for returns and exchanges on their products. These policies can vary from seller to seller, but generally include information on how to initiate a return or exchange, the time frame within which a return or exchange can be requested, and the conditions under which a return or exchange will be accepted. Some sellers may offer a full refund or exchange, while others may only offer store credit or a partial refund.
- **Cancellations:** The cancellations setting on Etsy allows sellers to set their policies for canceling orders. These policies can vary from seller to seller and can include information on the conditions under which a buyer can cancel an order and any fees that may be associated with the cancellation. Generally, sellers will allow cancellations within a certain timeframe after the order has been placed, such as within 24 hours or before the item has been shipped. Some sellers may also charge a cancellation fee, such as a restocking fee or a fee to cover the cost of any materials that have already been purchased for the item.
- **Privacy:** The Privacy settings on Etsy allow users to control how their personal information is collected, used, and shared on the platform. These settings include options for controlling the types of information that is shared with Etsy

and third-party partners, as well as options for managing communication preferences and account settings. In the Privacy settings, users can choose to limit the types of information that Etsy collects from them, such as browsing data or search queries.

- **Fixed Polices**: The Fixed Policies section in an Etsy seller's dashboard is a set of pre-written policy templates that sellers can use to quickly create and publish their store policies, such as their shipping, returns, and payment policies. These templates provide a basic framework for the seller to follow but can be customized to suit the specific needs of the seller and their business.

Production Partners: If you plan to use any graphic design or printing services in your Etsy sticker shop, you need to make sure you are including these companies in the Production Partners section. I have several Production Partners entered for my shop. Not only do I have them in the main Production Partners section, but I then choose which ones are specific for each listing. For example, if I purchased a graphic on Creative Fabrica and then had that graphic printed as a sticker on Sticker Mule, I would select both of those companies as the Production Partners when I listed that specific sticker.

Not adding Production Partners can mean a designer could file a trademark infringement complaint on your listing, even if you purchased the graphic legally. Unfortunately, many Etsy shops steal artwork and try to pass it off as their own, meaning artists and designers have to keep their eyes on the site to see if someone is selling their work. Keeping up with entering any Production Partners you use will protect your shop and listings.

Offsite Ads: The final section under **Settings** that you will want to attend to is Offsite Ads. These are the ads that Etsy places on sites such as Google, Instagram, Facebook, Pinterest, and more. Etsy covers the upfront costs for these ads; as a seller, you only pay when someone clicks on your ad and purchases an item from your shop.

If you sell under $10,000 within a calendar year, you can choose whether or not to opt into Offsite Ads. If you sell over $10,000 in a calendar year, you have no choice but to have your listings included in these ads.

I personally opt into Offsite Ads. After all, I only pay when the ad leads to a sale. With Etsy, such a competitive marketplace, I want to have the best chance to reach customers. And Offsite Ads help me do that. Note that you can opt out of these ads at any time if you choose to until you reach the $10,000 sales mark.

Community & Help: The options to customize your shop are updated periodically. You can keep up with all of Etsy's announcements as well as get help under the Community & Help section, which is linked in your Shop Manager.

Facebook Shops: The Facebook Shops option in your Etsy seller dashboard allows you to connect your Etsy shop with your Facebook account and create a shop on Facebook. This allows you to sell your products directly on Facebook, in addition to your Etsy shop.

With Facebook Shops, you can create a personalized online store on Facebook, where you can showcase your products and make them available for purchase. You can also create posts and ads on Facebook to promote your products and drive traffic to your shop.

By connecting your Etsy shop to Facebook, you can easily import your products, product information, and inventory to your Facebook shop. This can save you time and effort as you do not have to manually upload your products to Facebook.

Once connected, you can also sync your inventory and sales across both platforms, so you don't have to worry about stock levels or order fulfillment between the two. Please note that you need to have a Facebook page set up before you can create a shop and connect it to your Etsy shop. Also, Facebook has certain policies and guidelines to follow regarding the use of its platform for commerce, make sure you are familiar with them before using Facebook Shops.

To Recap: You can change and edit your shop's look and policies at any time, so don't ever feel that you are locked into a choice forever. In fact, it can be fun to freshen things up a bit from time to time. It's your Etsy sticker shop; enjoy the process of making it your own!

CHAPTER SEVEN: HOW TO LIST STICKERS ON ETSY

Once you have your Etsy shop set up, it's finally time to start listing your stickers for sale!

Listing items on Etsy can be a time-consuming process, as the platform offers many customization options for listings. These options allow sellers to provide detailed information about their products and make them more visible to potential buyers. However, the lengthy listing form can be overwhelming for new sellers, especially if they have many items to list.

There are several steps to complete within the Etsy listing form. To start the process, you will need to:

1. Click on the "Add a listing" icon in the top right corner of your "Shop Manager" page.
2. A new listing template titled "Add a new listing" will appear for you to fill out.

Photos: The first section of the Etsy listing form is for your photos. You can add up to 10 photos for each listing. It's ideal to provide as many photos as possible of the items you are selling. Many sticker sellers have photos of the stickers against a white background but then also show what the stickers will look like on planner pages, on water bottles and laptops, or in scrapbooks.

It's a good idea to include multiple photographs of your stickers in your listings to give potential buyers a clear idea of what they are purchasing. In addition to showing the stickers on various items to give a sense of scale and usage ideas, you can also include close-up shots of the stickers to showcase details and highlight any special features. The number of photographs you include will depend on the type of stickers you are selling and the amount of detail you want to show.

In general, it's a good idea to include at least one full-size photograph of each sticker and one or more additional photographs that show close-up details or highlight any special features. Keep in mind that Etsy allows up to 10 photographs per listing, so you have plenty of space to include a variety of images. Just be sure to choose high-quality photographs that accurately represent your stickers and avoid using any blurry or poorly lit images.

Instead of showing my stickers on products, I use a static wood background in Canva for my thumbnail photos and display the stickers against it. Each of my sticker listings typically includes a matte sticker, holographic sticker, and magnet version of the same design, so my thumbnail will show both the matte and holographic versions.

To give customers a good look at the difference between the matte and holographic versions of my stickers, I include separate photographs of each in my listings. I also use the photos separately later in the listing to help buyers know exactly which version they are purchasing. I'll cover showing variations of products later in this section.

Mockups: Some sellers choose to show their stickers on products, such as water bottles and laptops, to attract more customers. This can be done using mockups, which are pre-made images that allow you to display your stickers on various products without having to take the photos yourself. While I haven't needed to add more photos to sell my stickers, using mockups is a common practice among many sellers.

Mockups are pre-made images that allow you to digitally place your stickers on various products, such as water bottles, to showcase them in your listings. Many Etsy sellers offer mockup photos for sale, and you can easily find them by searching for "mockups" on the platform. If you need mockups of specific products, such as water bottles, you can also do a targeted search using relevant keywords.

Some Etsy sellers choose to pay for subscriptions to mockup websites to have access to a wide variety of mockup templates for different products. These mockups can be a useful tool for showcasing your products in a professional and visually appealing way and can be used in a variety of marketing materials, including your product listings, social media posts, and promotional materials.

Keep in mind that while mockups can be a useful way to showcase your products, they are not a substitute for high-quality product photographs. It's a good idea to include both mockups and real-life photographs of your products in your listings to give potential buyers the most accurate representation of what they are purchasing.

There are many mockup websites available, and the specific features and products offered can vary. Some common types of products that may be available on mockup websites include:

- **Product mockups:** These are digital representations of physical products that can be used to showcase your products in various settings or poses.
- **Scene generators:** These are templates that allow you to create custom product mockups by placing your products into pre-designed scenes or backgrounds.
- **Backgrounds and textures:** These are digital images that can be used to create custom backgrounds or add texture to your mockups.
- **Fonts and graphics:** These are digital design elements that can be used to add text or graphics to your mockups.

Many mockup websites offer a wide variety of mockup templates for different products. Some popular mockup websites include:

- **Creative Market:** Creative Market offers a wide range of mockup templates for products such as t-shirts, bags, business cards, and more.
- **Placeit:** Placeit is a mockup generator that allows you to create custom mockups using your designs. It offers a wide variety of mockup templates for products such as t-shirts, mugs, phone cases, and more.
- **The Mockup Club:** The Mockup Club is a website that offers a curated selection of high-quality mockup templates for products such as t-shirts, posters, business cards, and more.
- **Pixelbuddha:** Pixelbuddha is a website that offers a wide range of mockup templates for products such as t-shirts, business cards, and more.
- **Graphic Burger:** Graphic Burger is a website that offers a variety of free and premium mockup templates for products such as t-shirts, business cards, and more.

You can also hire graphic designers through websites such as Fiverr and Upwork to create custom mockups for you. This can be a good option if you want to create mockups that are specifically tailored to your products or branding. Many Etsy shops exclusively sell mockups. These shops typically offer a wide range of mockup templates for different products, such as t-shirts, business cards, and, of course, stickers.

Do you need mockups for your products? Honestly, that's a personal choice. Search Etsy for the type of stickers you plan on selling. If you are starting a planner sticker shop, search "planner sticker sheets" on Etsy, find the shops with the most sales, and look at their photos. If they are using mockups, you may consider doing so, too, or figure out how to take similar pictures yourself.

Thumbnail Photo: The thumbnail photo in your Etsy listing is the main image that appears for your listing on the platform. It's the first thing that customers will see when they come across your listing, so it's important to choose a high-quality and visually appealing thumbnail photo to grab their attention and entice them to click on your listing to learn more. After you upload all of the pictures you have for your listing, you can easily move them around, choosing the best one as your thumbnail photo.

Video: Etsy allows sellers to include a short video in their listings, which can be a great way to showcase their products and give shoppers a better understanding of what they are purchasing. Videos can be especially helpful for showing customers the size of your stickers as well as showing them the backside of your products.

To add a video to your Etsy listing, follow these stipes:

1. Go to the "Shop Manager" and click on the "Listings" tab.
2. Find the listing that you want to edit and click on the "Edit" button.
3. Scroll down to the "Photos" section.
4. Click on the "Add video" button.
5. Choose a video from your computer or device to upload.
6. Click the "Save" button to add the video to your listing.

It's important to note that adding a video to your Etsy listing can be a time-consuming process, as you will need to create and upload the video. With a time limit of only 15 seconds, it can be difficult to properly showcase your item in the time allotted. You will likely need several takes to end up with a video you are happy with.

Listing Details: After uploading photos for your Etsy listing, the next step is to fill in the listing details. This includes important information about your product such as its category, title, description, price, and availability. Providing as many details as possible can help shoppers to find and understand your product more easily and can also increase the chances of your listing being found in search results.

Title: The first field under Listing Details is for the title. A keyword-loaded title is essential for Etsy shoppers to find your listing when they are searching for the site. Etsy relies heavily on Search Engine Optimization (SEO) to bring shoppers not only to the website but also to individual shops.

SEO refers to the practice of optimizing your online content so that it is more visible and easily discoverable by search engines like Google. When done effectively, SEO can help your products to rank higher in search results and increase the chances of them being seen by potential customers. If you are new to Etsy and are not familiar with SEO, it can be helpful to learn some basic principles and best practices.

Here are a few tips for optimizing your Etsy listings for better visibility:

- Use relevant and specific keywords: Choose keywords that accurately describe your products and are commonly used by potential customers when searching for similar products.
- Use your keywords strategically: Use your keywords in your title, tags, and description to signal to search engines what your product is about.
- Use high-quality images: Use clear and attractive images of your products to help them stand out in search results and attract potential customers.
- Use descriptive titles and descriptions: Use descriptive and informative titles and descriptions to give shoppers a clear understanding of your products and their features and benefits.

The title of your Etsy listing is an important part of your product's SEO, as it helps to signal to search engines and shoppers what your product is about. By including relevant keywords in your title, you can increase the chances that your product will be found by potential customers who are searching for similar products.

Simply typing "Planner Sticker Sheets" as your title isn't enough. You need to put in as many keywords or short phrases (referred to as long-tail keywords) into your title that relate to the item you're selling.

But what else can you say about planner sticker sheets? Isn't that all they are? The answer is no. When it comes to selling on Etsy, there are numerous ways to describe items. For planner sticker sheets, common keywords to use are:

- Planner stickers
- Sticker sheet
- Sticker sheets
- Stickers
- Planner
- Journal Stickers
- Planner sticker
- Cute stickers
- Functional stickers
- Sticker
- Planner sticker sheet
- Scrapbook stickers
- Small stickers
- Decorative stickers
- Calendar stickers
- Reminder stickers

If your stickers have special identifying features, you'll want to include those, including things such as size, color, occasion, holiday, and even who the target customer is for that particular listing.

A quick Etsy search of "planner sticker sheets will bring up over 100,000 results. You read that right: over one hundred THOUSAND! And new listings are constantly being created.

On the day of this writing, the top-selling planner sticker sheet was from a store called TheCozyComfyHome, a shop that boosts over 30,000 sales. Here is the title for one of their sticker sheets: "Planner Stickers, Planner Sticker Sheet, Pretty Boho Neutral Color, Aesthetic Matte Stickers, Chores Icons, Trash Recycle Vacuum."

See how commas are separating each keyword phrase? The commas act to separate each keyword or keyword phrase that customers may type into Etsy's search bar.

But how can you find the best keywords for your Etsy sticker listings? Most Etsy sellers, including myself, use software to research keywords, not just for titles but also for descriptions and tags. I discussed a few of these sites in Chapter Two of this book if you would like to refer back to the chapter for the list.

I prefer EtsyCheck.com's Keyword Trend tool to research the best keywords for my titles. I simply type in a basic sticker description, such as a "pug dog sticker" and review the results they give me. I choose a mix of the most popular keywords along with some that aren't as common to give my listing the best chance of being found.

About this listing: When creating a new listing on Etsy, you will need to provide information about your product in the "About this listing" section. This includes details such as the type of product you are selling (finished product or crafting supply), the quantity of the product you have available, and the processing time for your orders. Providing this information can help shoppers to understand what you are selling and how it can be used and can also help them to make informed decisions about whether to purchase your product.

Who made it?

- I did
- A member of my shop
- Another company or person

What is it?

- A finished product
- A supply or tool to make things

When was it made?

- Not yet made (meaning the item is made to order)
- Recently (within the past ten years)
- Vintage (20 years or longer)

Category: There are several sticker categories and subcategories on Etsy, most of which are under the Craft Supplies & Tools section. including:

- Paper & Party Supplies: Paper: Sticker, Labels & Tags: Stickers
- Paper & Party Supplies: Paper: Sticker, Labels & Tags: Bumper Stickers
- Paper & Party Supplies: Paper: Sticker, Labels & Tags: Labels
- Paper & Party Supplies: Paper: Sticker, Labels & Tags: Seals
- Paper & Party Supplies: Paper: Sticker, Labels & Tags: Address & Shipping Labels
- Paper & Party Supplies: Paper: Sticker, Labels & Tags: Sets
- Craft Supplies & Tools: Paper, Party & Kids: Papercraft: Scrapbooking: Embellishments: Stickers

Etsy will pre-select a category based on your Title. And while they are usually right, sometimes their selection is completely wrong. For example, they will usually put Christmas tree skirts under women's skirts.

Regardless of what Etsy may pre-select as your product category, go ahead and type in exactly what you are selling. To use the example we've been working with, typing "planner stickers" into the Category bar will bring up several options, most under the Paper & Party Supply category but also likely under Office & School Supplies.

You want to select the category that is most relevant to the product you are selling. However, since most of the sticker subcategories are under one main category, in the end, Etsy will populate your listing with multiple sections.

As an example, if you choose to have your planner sticker sheets listed under

"Calendars & Planners," Etsy will put your listing into that category as well as several others, including "Paper & Party Supplies," "Paper," "Books," and "Books Movies & Music."

My vinyl stickers are almost always in "Paper & Party Supplies," "Paper," "Stickers Labels & Tags, and Stickers."

Craft type: Depending on which category you choose for the item you are listing, "Craft type" options may appear for you. This is an optional section but choose all the options presented to you as this will put your product in more categories for shoppers to find. As an example, Etsy suggests that my vinyl stickers go into "Card making & stationery," "Kid's crafts," "Party & gifts," and "Scrapbooking."

Material: Depending on which product category you choose for the item you are listing; "Material" is another option section that may appear within your listing template. If the material of the stickers you are selling is offered from the drop-down menu, select it. For stickers, paper is one of the choices. Note that since I sell vinyl stickers, which are different from paper stickers, I do not choose paper. Again, this category is optional. There is another option for entering additional materials further down in the listing template.

Primary color & Secondary color: Two optional categories that may appear depending on the category you are listing in are both "Primary color" and "Secondary color." Etsy notes that "Primary and secondary color attributes are interchangeable so you can show shoppers that your item is multicolored. Skip secondary color if your item is only one color."

Width & Height: Two optional categories that may appear depending on the category you are listing are "Width" and "Height." You can choose to enter measurements in centimeters, feet, inches, meters, millimeters, or yards. Note that if you are selling planner stickers or sticker sheets, you'll want to distinguish whether your measurements are for the sheets themselves or the size of the individual stickers. If you are concerned that customers might mistake the size of a sticker sheet for the size of a single sticker, you can skip this section and instead provide clarification on your measurements in the "Description" field.

Set: Depending on the product category you choose, "Set" might be presented to you as an optional category. A set simply refers to if more than one item is included in the sale. For instance, I sell a handful of sticker packs that contain anywhere from two to four individual stickers. I list these as "Sets".

However, if you are selling sticker sheets, note that each sheet is considered one item. Many planner sticker shops offer bundles of several sticker sheets together. In that instance, they would list these bundles as "Sets" as the customer will be receiving multiple sheets.

While there are multiple stickers on each sheet, each sheet itself refers to ONE item.

Occasion: Depending on your product category, a field for "Occasion" might be in your listing template. It is usually included when you are listing stickers in any category, so you will likely see this field. Occasions you may see, depending on the category, include:

- 1st birthday
- Anniversary
- Baby shower
- Bachelor party
- Bachelorette party
- Back to school
- Baptism
- Bar & Bat Mitzvah
- Birthday
- Bridal shower
- Confirmation
- Divorce & breakup
- Engagement
- First Communion
- Graduation
- Grief & mourning
- Housewarming
- LGBTQ pride
- Moving
- Pet loss
- Prom
- Quinceanera & Sweet 16
- Retirement
- Wedding

Etsy describes the "Occasion" field this way: "Add to items designed for the occasion, for example, graduation party décor, not for items that could be gifted for an occasion. You can skip this attribute if it isn't relevant."

I ignore Etsy's advice here and try to select an occasion for all my listings, regardless of whether it is décor or a gift. For example, I might select "Wedding" for a Valentine's Sticker.

Holiday: Occasions are different than designated holidays, hence why Etsy offers "Holiday" as an option for sticker listings. Holidays you may see as options include:

- April Fools'
- Christmas
- Cinco de Mayo
- Diwali
- Easter
- Eid
- Father's Day
- Halloween
- Hanukkah
- Holi
- Independence Day
- Kwanzaa
- Lunar New Year
- Mother's Day
- New Year's
- Passover
- St. Patrick's Day
- Thanksgiving
- Valentine's Day
- Veterans Day

Etsy describes this section as follows: "Add to items meant specifically for a holiday, for example, a Mother's Day card, not for items that could be gifted for a holiday. You can skip this attribute if it isn't relevant."

Just as I do for the "Occasion" section, I ignore Etsy's advice and add a "Holiday" if I feel one suits the sticker I am listing. For example, I would list a "Cat Mom" sticker in the Mother's Day category, even though it isn't a holiday-specific item.

Theme: Another optional field that appears in most sticker categories is "Theme." When I am listing a vinyl sticker, the listing template will typically offer me the following themes:

- Animals
- Beach & Tropical
- Bugs & insects
- Evil eye
- Fall
- Fantasy & Sci-Fi
- Floral
- Food & drink
- Geometric
- Infinity
- Keys & locks
- Letters & words
- Love & Friendship
- Luck
- Music
- Nautical
- Patriotic & flags
- People
- Plants & trees
- Punk & tattoos

- Religious
- Science & tech
- Southwestern
- Sports & Fitness
- Spring
- Stars & celestial
- Steampunk
- Summer
- Travel & Transportation
- Western & cowboy
- Winter
- Zodiac

PRO TIP: The "Occasion", "Holiday", and "Theme" lists offer a great way to get inspiration for new stickers. After all, Etsy has included these sections because shoppers are searching for any buying products that fall under each. I like to find an occasion or holiday and match it with a theme. For instance, I have several pet parent-themed stickers, such as "Pug Mom". For my "Pug Mom" stickers, I choose "Birthday" under "Occasion", "Mother's Day" under "Holiday", and "Animals" under "Theme."

Renewal options: You have the option to set your Etsy listings to automatically renew every four months for a fee of 20 cents per renewal, or you can choose to manually renew them. If you choose automatic renewal, your listing will be automatically renewed every four months and your account will be charged the renewal fee. If you choose manual renewal, your listing will expire after four months and you will need to manually relist it on Etsy if you want to continue selling the item. It's important to note that the renewal fee is in addition to any other fees you may be charged for listing and selling your item on Etsy.

I choose "Manual" renewal when I list a new sticker for sale. That way, after four months, I can reevaluate the listing. If the sticker hasn't been selling, I can take a second look at it and perhaps improve the listing. I may redo the title, research new tags, and make sure all relevant fields, even the optional ones, are selected.

If I have a sticker that has been selling well that ends after four months, when I relist it, I will change the "Renewal" option to "Automatic". Since it's proven to be a best-selling sticker, I want it to remain listed so that there is no disruption to its being active in my Etsy shop.

PRO TIP: If your Etsy sticker listing expires after four months, in addition to reevaluating the listing itself, it's a good time to take inventory of that product to make sure you have the correct quantity listed. I once had an in-demand sticker go out of stock. Since the listing also had magnets available in the same design, I didn't realize the sticker was out of stock until the listing ended automatically. I had to reorder and wait for the stickers to arrive before I could relist the sticker option, meaning I lost out on sales.

Type: Most sticker shops on Etsy sell physical stickers, such as planner sticker sheets or vinyl stickers, which are shipped to the customer. However, some sticker shops may also offer digital downloads of sticker templates that customers can use to print the stickers themselves. If your shop is selling physical stickers that will be shipped to the customer, you should choose the "Physical" option. If your shop is selling digital downloads of sticker templates, you should choose the "Digital" option.

Description: I have a confession: The description fields on the various websites I sell on often overwhelm me. Whether I'm creating a listing on Amazon for one of my books or a listing on eBay for a vintage collectible, I always get tripped up when it comes time to write the description. Should I just include the basic information? Should I include everything possible? Should I try to "sell" the item by telling the customer exactly why they should buy it?

I used to write as much as possible in my listing descriptions for fear of leaving out an important detail. But as the years have gone on and eBay, for instance, has added more description fields to their listing templates, I find myself writing very little in the description box and relying on the product specifics.

However, things are different on Etsy. On Etsy, the search engine optimization (SEO) process is different from other platforms like eBay. For your products to rank higher in Etsy's search results, you need to include relevant keywords in the title, description, and tags of your listings. This means that all the keywords you include in the title of your listing should also be present in the description. Using the right keywords in all these areas can help improve the visibility of your products on Etsy and attract more potential buyers to your shop.

Does this mean you copy and paste your "Title" into your "Description" as is? No. Instead of simply copying and pasting the title of your listing into the description, you should use the keywords from the title in a sentence to describe your product. For example, if your title is "Christmas Stickers, Christmas Planner Sticker Sheets, Holiday Planner Stickers," you could rewrite it in the description as: "This set of Christmas planner sticker sheets is perfect for all of your holiday planning needs. The stickers are great for adding a festive touch to your planner or journal." This helps to provide more information about your product and makes the description more informative and engaging for potential buyers.

Does this seem like a lot of extra work? Yes, it does and it is. And I will be honest in telling you that I don't always write this much in my Etsy listing. Because while Etsy will tell you that this is what you need to do for your listings to be found in their search, it's honestly extremely time-consuming. Rather, I take the "do the best you can" approach for my Etsy descriptions. I make sure my title and tags are loaded with keywords, but I give myself a bit of grace when it comes to the description.

First off, I make sure all relevant information is in my description. Here is an example of the description for one of my best-selling stickers:

- Fun STICKERS & MAGNETS of London, England icons!
- The London Eye, Big Ben, London Bridge, Palace Guard, Double Decker Bus, Red Phone Booth, Crown, and Teapot with Teacup
- 3"
- Die-cut
- Vinyl
- Waterproof
- Heat-safe
- Scratch resistant
- Perfect for water bottles, laptops, refrigerators, and even cars!

Is this the best description ever written? Far from it! This was one of my earliest listings, but this design is one of my best sellers. I made sure to include the most important information, which for stickers is the size, if they are vinyl, if they are waterproof, and how the stickers can be used. Could I have included a lot more information? Yes. Have I? No. Yet because of the sticker design, the title, and the tags, this sticker sells well. When I first listed this sticker, I took the "best I could do" strategy with the description and then moved on to listing other products.

That being said, here are several ways to optimize the SEO of an Etsy listing description:

- Use variations of your keywords in the description. For

example, if your main keyword is "handmade ceramic mug," you could also include variations such as "ceramic coffee mug" or "handmade mug."

- Keep the description concise and to the point. Avoid using fluff or filler words that do not add value to the description.
- Use bullet points to highlight key features and benefits of the product. This makes it easier for potential customers to quickly scan the description and understand what the product offers.
- Include a call to action in the description. This could be something like "Add to cart now" or "Contact us for custom orders." This can encourage potential customers to take action and make a purchase.

Production partners: Etsy Production Partners is a program offered by Etsy that connects shop owners with manufacturing partners who can help them produce and fulfill orders for their products. The program is designed to help shop owners scale their businesses and meet the demand for their products without having to handle production and fulfillment themselves.

To become a production partner, a manufacturer must apply and be accepted into the program by Etsy. Once accepted, they can begin working with Etsy shop owners to produce and fulfill orders for their products. Shop owners can then use the Production Partners dashboard on Etsy to manage their orders and track the production and fulfillment process.

Etsy Production Partners can help shop owners save time and resources by allowing them to focus on the creative aspects of their business, such as product design and marketing, while the production partner handles the manufacturing and fulfillment of their products. This can also help shop owners reach more customers and grow their businesses.

I currently have four production partners linked to my Etsy account. If you use a production partner, you must link them to your shop as failure to do so could result in a designer filing a trademark violation against you. Most production partner names are hidden from shoppers; they will only see a message that you as the seller created the product with the help of outside companies.

Section: Etsy allows sellers to create "sections" in their Etsy shops, which is their term for "store categories". This is a great feature to not only help you categorize your items and to help shoppers better search your shop, but how you title your sections is another form of SEO.

Even if you are only selling one type of product, such as planner sticker sheets or vinyl stickers, you can still create separate sections for the different themes of stickers or different demographics. For instance, I sell a wide variety of stickers that I group into different shop sections, including "Food & Beverage," "Pets & Animals," and "Retro & Vintage."

Naming my Etsy shop sections with the same terms I use in the titles and descriptions of my listings creates another level of SEO to help my stickers show up high in Etsy's search. If I list a strawberry sticker as a food-themed sticker in both the title and description, add "food sticker" as a tag, and then add it to the "Food & Beverage" section of my shop, my listing will have a good chance of being shown up high in search when someone searches for food, fruit, and strawberry stickers.

You can create up to 20 sections in your Etsy shop, and you can edit them at any time. You can also arrange them how you want them to be listed in your shop. I arrange mine alphabetically.

Tags: Etsy tags are words or phrases that sellers can add to their listings to help buyers find their products. These tags help to categorize the items and make them easier to search for on the platform. For example, a seller of handmade jewelry might use tags such as "handmade," "silver," and "turquoise" to describe their products. By using relevant tags, sellers can increase the visibility of their listings and make it more likely that they will appear in search results. Additionally, Etsy uses these tags to help surface relevant items to buyers when they are browsing the platform.

When choosing Etsy tags for your sticker listings, it's important to consider the words and phrases that buyers might use when searching for products like yours. This can help to increase the visibility of your listings and make it more likely that they will appear in search results. In addition to using relevant keywords that describe your stickers, such as their materials, colors, and style, you can also consider using tags that relate to the theme or purpose of your stickers.

For example, if you are selling stickers with a nature theme, you might use tags such as "outdoor," "floral," or "forest." It's also a good idea to use a combination of broad and specific tags to maximize your chances of being found in search results. For example, you might use a broad tag such as "stickers" as well as more specific tags such as "vinyl stickers," "planner stickers," or "water bottle stickers."

Here are some tips for choosing effective Etsy tags:

- **Use a mix of broad and specific tags.** For example, you might use a broad tag like "stickers" for all of your listings, but also include more specific tags such as "vinyl sticker" or "waterproof sticker" for individual items. This will help buyers to find your products when searching for a specific type of sticker, as well as when browsing more generally.
- **Include relevant keywords.** It is important to include relevant keywords in your tags to help buyers find your products when searching for specific materials, styles, or colors. By using descriptive and accurate tags, you can

increase the chances of your products appearing in search results and being seen by potential buyers. For example, if you sell planner stickers, you might include tags such as "planner stickers," "sticker sheets," or "planning" to describe the materials and style of your products. You can also use tags to describe the colors or patterns of your stickers, such as "red," "striped," or "boho."

- **Consider using popular search terms.** It's a good idea to do some research to find out what search terms are most commonly used on Etsy. You can do this by using the Etsy search bar and looking at the suggestions that appear as you type. This can give you an idea of the words and phrases that buyers are using when searching for products like yours.
- **Use all 13 available tags.** Etsy allows sellers to add up to 13 tags to each listing. Be sure to use all of these tags, as this will give your products more chances to appear in search results.
- **Avoid using irrelevant or misleading tags.** It's important to avoid using tags that don't accurately describe your product, as this can be misleading to buyers. Additionally, using irrelevant tags can hurt your chances of appearing in search results, as Etsy's search algorithm is designed to surface relevant products to buyers.

When choosing Etsy tags for your stickers, you should consider using a mix of broad and specific tags that accurately describe your product. For example, you might include tags such as "planner stickers," "stickers," "handmade," and "vinyl." Additionally, you should consider using relevant keywords that describe the designs or themes of your stickers, such as "weekly," "monthly," "to-do list," or "habit tracker."

Here are some other potential Etsy tags for planner stickers:

- planner stickers

- planner sticker sheet
- planner sticker sets
- sticker sheet
- organization
- agenda
- stationery
- decorative
- graphic design
- sticker pack
- functional
- scrapbooking
- bullet journal

Here are some other potential Etsy tags for planner stickers:

- Vinyl stickers
- Waterproof stickers
- Water bottle stickers
- Decals
- Laptop stickers
- Car stickers
- Phone case stickers
- Wall stickers
- Window stickers

Regardless of the type of sticker you are listing – planner or vinyl – be sure to add tags that relate to the design. Using the example, I gave earlier of me listing a pug dog sticker, these are the tags I used:

1. Sticker
2. Vinyl sticker
3. Waterproof sticker
4. Water bottle sticker

5. Laptop sticker
6. Decals
7. Pugs
8. Pug dogs
9. Pug stickers
10. Dog stickers
11. Cute stickers
12. Pet stickers
13. Animal stickers

PRO TIP: Even when you are listing similar items, try to change up your tags. Using different tags for your listings widens your reach when customers are searching Etsy for the products they want. And if they find one of your listings, they might click through to your shop to see everything you have for sale.

IMPORTANT: Just as you cannot use trademarked images and text in your sticker designs, you also cannot use them in your tags. If you sell planner stickers, you cannot use "Happy Planner" or "Erin Condren" as tags, nor the names of the top Etsy sticker shops.

Materials: The materials field in Etsy listings is a section where sellers can specify the materials used to make their product, whether it is handmade or not. Note that this is a different field than the "Material" section that appears earlier in the listing. The "Material" section features a drop-down menu with limited options. The "Materials" section allows you to type in words.

Just as with tags, you can enter up to 13 materials for each listing. A site such as EtsyCheck.com can not only generate tags for you but also materials. Because "vinyl" is not an option in the "Material" section, I enter it in the "Materials" field in my listings.

Inventory & Pricing: The next section of an Etsy listing is "Inventory & Pricing". For stickers, you will need to fill out the following:

Price: Etsy reminds sellers to "factor in the costs of materials, labor, and other business expenses. If you offer free shipping, make sure to include the cost of the shipping so it doesn't eat into your profits."

If you are only offering one product in a listing, such as a sticker sheet set or one vinyl sticker, you can enter a single price. However, if you are offering several different items within one listing, for instance, a choice of sticker sheets or different sizes of the same vinyl sticker design, you will want to scroll down the listing field to the "Variations" section. I offer almost all my stickers in matte and holographic, and I also offer magnets. Since most of my listings feature three versions, I list them using under "variations."

I'll cover "variations" in a moment, but first, let's continue as if you are only listing one product in a listing. You'll already set the "price," and next is the "quantity."

Quantity: The quantity section in an Etsy listing is where you specify how many units of your product you have available for sale. To fill out the quantity section of your Etsy listing, enter the number of units you have available for sale in the "Quantity" field. It's important to keep your quantity up to date so that buyers know if the product is in stock and can make informed purchasing decisions. If you run out of stock, you can either restock the item or set the quantity to zero to indicate that it is currently out of stock.

Etsy automatically tracks the number of items listed for sale in a shop and decreases the available quantity as items are purchased. This helps to ensure that the seller does not oversell an item. When a customer makes a purchase, the available quantity is reduced by the number of items purchased. If the available quantity reaches 0, the item will be marked as "sold out" and will no longer be available for purchase until the seller restocks the item and updates the quantity.

PRO TIP: I list one or two fewer of each sticker I have on hand. If I have 20 of one design, I will list 19. That way I am covered if I discover that one is defective or if I accidentally miscount. This protects me from having to cancel an order.

SKU: A SKU (Stock Keeping Unit) is a unique identifier that is used to track and manage inventory in a retail or e-commerce setting. In an Etsy listing, the SKU is a field where you can enter a unique identifier for your product. This is typically a combination of letters and numbers that you assign to each product or variation in your inventory.

You do not need to fill out the SKU field in an Etsy listing, but it can be useful if you have a large inventory and want to track your products using a unique identifier. For example, you might use an SKU to keep track of different variations of your product (e.g., different sizes or colors) or to distinguish between different versions of your product (e.g., an original design vs. a limited-edition design).

If you decide to use an SKU in your Etsy listing, it's a good idea to make sure that it is unique and easy to remember. This will make it easier for you to manage your inventory and for your customers to identify specific products.

Here are some potential ways to create SKUs for your Etsy sticker shop:

- Use a combination of letters and numbers to represent the product's design and size. For example, if you have a sticker that features a penguin design and is 3 inches wide, you might use the SKU "PENG3."
- Include the product's color in the SKU. For example, if you have a sticker that features a cat design and is available in both

black and white, you might use the SKUs "CATB" and "CATW" for the black and white versions, respectively.

- Use a code that represents the product's theme or category. For example, if you have a sticker that belongs to your "Nature" collection, you might use the SKU "NAT1" or "NAT2" for the first and second stickers in that collection, respectively.

Once you have a system in place, you can apply it to all of your products and start using the SKUs in your Etsy listings. To add an SKU to a listing, scroll down to the "Inventory" section and enter the SKU in the designated field. This will help you to keep track of your products and manage your inventory more effectively.

Restock requests: The optional restock request section in an Etsy listing is a feature that allows buyers to request that an out-of-stock item be restocked. If you have enabled this feature for your listing, buyers will be able to enter their email addresses to receive a notification when the item becomes available again.

To enable the restock request feature for your Etsy listing, go to the "Edit" page for the listing and scroll down to the "Restock request" section. Here, you can toggle the "Allow customers to request a restock" option to "On." When this option is enabled, a "Notify me when available" button will appear on your listing page for out-of-stock items.

Using the restock request feature can be a good way to keep in touch with interested buyers and potentially generate additional sales when an item becomes available again. However, it's important to note that enabling this feature does not guarantee that you will restock the item, and you are not required to fulfill restock requests.

Variations: The above steps were for if you were only listing one product in your listing. The following steps are if you want to offer more than one type or style of product within the same listings:

1. Scroll down to the "Variations" section and click the "Add a variation" button.
2. Select the option you want to add as a variation (e.g., "Size," "Color," "Style").
3. Enter the different options for the variation. For example, if you're offering stickers in three different sizes, you would enter "Small," "Medium," and "Large" as options for the "Size" variation.
4. Set the price and quantity for each variation. If the price or quantity is the same for all variations, you can use the "Same as main listing" option. If the price or quantity is different for each variation, you can enter the values individually.
5. Repeat this process for any additional variations you want to offer.
6. Click on the "link photos" tab to assign photos to each variation. Even if all of the options look the same (for instance, it is the same sticker but in different sizes), I still link to a photo. The photos available are the same ones you added at the top of the listing.

It may be beneficial to create separate listings for each product you sell on Etsy. For example, I have images available such as matte stickers, holographic stickers, and magnets. When I first started my sticker shop, I would list all three options in the same listing. However, I recently started separating the stickers into one listing and the magnets into another. This not only helps shoppers who are searching for stickers or magnets to more easily find my listings (as stickers and magnets are different categories on Etsy), but it also helps me keep better track of inventory. I could take it a step further and list the holographic stickers separately.

If you are offering "variations", you would include the quantity for each type of product. Sometimes I have 10 matte stickers, 50 holographic stickers, and 75 magnets available for the same design, all under the same listing.

Personalization: After you've completed the "Inventory & Pricing" section, the next field in the listing form is for "Personalization," which is an optional section where sellers can provide information about how their product can be personalized. This is, of course, only for products that can be customized, whether with a name, initials, dates, or other details chosen by the buyer.

When you turn on "Personalization" within your listing, you will see two fields: "Instructions for buyers" and "What the buyer will see." Note that you can offer personalization but also make it optional here. For example, you may offer a sticker that can be printed with our without a name on it. It would be up to the buyer to decide whether to include their personalization details or to leave this section blank as they want the sticker as is with no name.

The personalization field is different from the "Notes to Seller" field, which is where buyers can enter specific instructions or requests for the seller. The personalization field is used to provide information about the options available for personalizing the product, whereas the "Notes to Seller" field is used for buyers to provide specific instructions for their orders.

Shipping: Shipping orders for an online store can be intimidating for new sellers and setting up shipping for an Etsy shop is no exception. I will cover shipping extensively in the next chapter, but I will be going over the basics here.

If you are starting an Etsy sticker shop and have never shipped an order before, it's natural to feel anxious about the shipping process. However, Etsy has made it easy for sellers to set up shipping for their products. All you need to do is make a few decisions in the "Shipping" field of your listings to complete the setup process.

All orders on Etsy are shipped through the United States Postal Service (USPS). However, there are different shipping methods available, and the best one for your stickers will depend on their weight. For stickers, most sellers will be looking at packages weighing less than one pound, so they will likely ship their orders via First Class. First Class is a cost-effective shipping option for lightweight packages and is suitable for most sticker orders. There are two different categories for First Class: mail, which is when you put a stamp on a letter; and parcel, which is when packages are larger than stamps will cover.

I use First Class Mail to ship my orders of one vinyl sticker. Instead of hand addressing the envelope and attaching a stamp, I use Etsy's shipping label feature to print out a label with tracking. This is convenient and efficient. First Class Mail is the shipping method I use for envelopes that weigh four ounces or less and have a thickness of fewer than .25 inches. It's a reliable and cost-effective option for shipping lightweight packages like my vinyl stickers.

If a package weighs more than four ounces or is thicker than .25 inches, I use First Class Parcel as the shipping method. This is necessary for orders that are larger or heavier than what First Class Mail can accommodate. Although most of my orders are for a single sticker, I do occasionally get orders for multiple stickers and magnets.

To ensure that I'm using the correct shipping method, I keep a digital postage scale at my desk and weigh the items before shipping. If the order weighs more than four ounces, I put the items in a small poly bubble mailer instead of a card stock envelope. This helps to ensure that the package meets the requirements for First Class Parcel shipping.

To create shipping profiles on Etsy, follow these steps:

1. Go to your Shop Manager and click on the "Settings" tab.
2. Click on the "Shipping & Payments" option in the menu on the left side of the page.
3. In the "Shipping profiles" section, click on the "Add a new shipping profile" button.
4. Enter a name for your shipping profile and select the countries you want to ship to.
5. Enter the details for your shipping options, including the destination, cost, and any additional handling fees or processing times.
6. Click "Save" to add the shipping profile to your shop.

You can create multiple shipping profiles for different destinations or different types of items in your shop. For example, you could create a separate shipping profile for domestic and international shipments or different sizes and weights of items. To use a shipping profile, you will need to select it when you create a listing for an item in your shop.

I use Etsy's "FREE Under 4 Pounds (No Media)" shipping profile for all of my stickers. This option allows me to offer "free" shipping to my customers because I include the cost of shipping in the price of my stickers. It's important to note that there is no such thing as truly free shipping, as someone has to pay for the postage. In this case, I factor the cost of shipping into the price of my stickers so that my customers don't have to pay for them separately. This works well for me because it allows me to offer a convenient and hassle-free shipping experience to my customers while still covering my shipping costs.

However, I don't just use one of Etsy's Shipping Profiles as they are set. I like to customize them to meet my needs. To edit a Shipping Profile, I click on the "Edit" button next to the profile. This brings up a new screen where I can make various changes to the profile. For example, I can edit the name of the profile, specify the countries where I'm willing to ship, and set the shipping rates for different regions. I can also choose whether I want to offer free shipping, flat rate shipping, or calculate shipping based on the weight of the package. By editing my Shipping Profiles, I can ensure that my shipping options are tailored to my business needs and are easy for my customers to understand.

Processing time: The processing time is the length of time it takes for me to prepare, package, and mail out an order after a customer places it. I have my processing time set to 1-2 business days, which means that I ship out orders the next business day after they come in. This allows me to get orders out to my customers as quickly as possible and helps to ensure that they receive their items promptly. I try to be as efficient as possible when it comes to processing orders so that my customers are satisfied with their shopping experience.

It's important to be honest about your processing time and only promise a fast turnaround if you can deliver on that promise. If you set your processing time to a reasonable amount of time that you can consistently meet, you can help to manage your customers' expectations and build trust in your business.

If you aren't able to meet the promised processing time, the customer may choose to cancel the order if they no longer wish to wait for the item. Etsy may take action if a seller is consistently unable to process orders within the promised processing time and is causing frustration for their customers. This could include issuing a warning to the seller or even suspending their account if the problem persists. Etsy sellers need to be timely and efficient when it comes to processing orders to ensure a positive experience for their customers. After all, an unhappy customer may not only decide not to shop from you, but they may also decide not to shop on Etsy at all. And that decision hurts the site as a whole.

Where I'll Ship: In the "Shipping" section of your listing, you can specify the countries that you are willing to ship to. I personally only ship within the United States, as international shipping, even to Canada, can be very expensive and may not be cost-effective for my business.

However, many Etsy sellers do offer international shipping and may find it to be a viable option for their business. Ultimately, the decision to ship internationally or not is up to you as the seller and will depend on your business model, the products you offer, and the costs associated with international shipping. It's important to carefully consider these factors and decide what works best for you and your business.

If you choose to offer international shipping, click on the "Edit" button next to the shipping profile you want to use. In the "Shipping Profile" window that appears, click on the "Add countries" button. From the drop-down menu, select the countries that you are willing to ship to. You can choose individual countries or select a group of countries from the menu. Once you have selected all of the countries that you want to include, click on the "Save" button. Your Etsy listing will now be set up for international shipping to the countries that you selected.

It's important to specify the shipping rates for each country or region that you are willing to ship to when setting up international shipping for your Etsy listings. You can do this by clicking on the "Add shipping rates" button and entering the rates for each destination. Alternatively, you can choose calculated shipping and let Etsy automatically determine the rates based on the weight of your item. This can be a convenient option if you don't want to manually enter rates for each country.

Keep in mind that if a customer purchases two or more items from you in the same order, the weights of the items will be combined to calculate the shipping cost. It's a good idea to be aware of this when setting your shipping rates, as it can affect the cost of shipping for orders with multiple items.

Shipping Services: Etsy offers shipping through the United States Postal Service (USPS) and provides several options for sellers to choose from. These options include First Class and Priority Mail, as well as Media Mail and Parcel Select Ground.

First Class Mail is a cost-effective option for lightweight packages and is suitable for most small to medium-sized items. It typically takes 1-3 business days for First Class Mail to be delivered within the United States. Most sticker shops ship packages weighing under four ounces via First Class Mail.

First Class Package is a shipping option for packages that are more than four ounces but weigh less than 16 ounces. For sticker orders weighing over four ounces, I ship via First Class Package. I have small bubble mailers that I use for these orders, which are larger and heavier than orders of just one or two stickers.

Priority Mail is a faster shipping option that typically takes 1-3 business days for delivery within the United States. It's a good choice for larger or heavier items, or for those that need to be delivered more quickly. Priority Mail is for packages weighing over one pound. You only need to enter the weight range for Priority. For example, one to two pounds, two to three pounds, etc. You do not need to enter the exact weight down to the ounce. You can order free USPS Priority Mail shipping supplies, including envelopes and boxes, online at store.usps.com/store. Your mail carrier will deliver these supplies free to your home.

Media Mail is a shipping option specifically for media items like books, CDs, and DVDs. It's a cost-effective option for these types of items, but it may take longer for Media Mail to be delivered than other shipping methods.

Parcel Select Ground is a ground shipping option that is generally more economical than other options, but it may take longer for delivery. It's a good choice for large or heavy items that don't need to be delivered quickly. As with Priority Mail, Parcel Select is for packages weighing over one pound. You only need to enter the weight range for Parcel packages. For example, one to two pounds, two to three pounds, etc. You do not need to enter the exact weight down to the ounce.

Note that while you can use Priority Mail boxes for Priority Mail packages, you cannot use these USPS-branded Priority Mail envelopes or boxes for First Class Package, Media Mail, or Parcel Post. Most Etsy sticker shops do the majority of their shipping via First Class and ship orders in envelopes and bubble mailers, so you may never need to use these other services.

Free Shipping: If you want to offer free shipping to your customers, you can choose the "Free" shipping profile option when setting up your Etsy listings. This option allows you to offer free shipping to domestic (within the United States) and/or international destinations.

Keep in mind that while free shipping can be a great way to attract customers, it's important to consider the cost of shipping when setting your prices. If you offer free shipping, you'll need to factor in the cost of shipping into the price of your products.

Many sellers who offer free domestic shipping do not offer free international shipping due to the high costs associated with international shipping. If you decide to offer free international shipping, you'll need to carefully consider the costs and make sure that it's financially viable for your business. It may be more cost-effective to offer discounted international shipping rather than offering it for free.

I offer "free" domestic shipping on all of my stickers, but I do so by building the cost of shipping into the price of my stickers. Since most of my sales are for single stickers, my margins are very tight. But by offering "free shipping", my listings show up higher in Etsy's search. The increased views lead to more sales, which helps me to offset the cost of covering postage.

Handling Fee: As an Etsy seller, you have the option to charge a handling fee to each order if you wish. This fee is typically added to the shipping cost and is visible to the customer as part of their total shipping charge. Handling fees can be used to cover the cost of materials or other expenses associated with preparing and shipping orders. If you are offering free shipping to your customers, adding a handling fee isn't an option as you've already told customers that their shipping costs are covered.

However, if you are charging the customer for shipping, you may choose to add a handling fee to cover your costs. Keep in mind that charging a separate handling fee in addition to the cost of shipping may not be well-received by customers, as it can make your products appear more expensive. Some customers may choose to shop elsewhere if they feel that the shipping and handling fees are too high. Instead of charging a separate handling fee, you may find it more effective to include your costs in the price of your products and offer competitive shipping rates to your customers.

Item Weight: It's a good idea to weigh your items before listing them on Etsy so that you can accurately specify the weight in your listings. This is particularly important for determining the shipping cost, as the weight of the item is a major factor in determining the cost of shipping.

If you are selling stickers, you'll want to weigh them to determine their weight. For example, if your vinyl stickers weigh less than one ounce when placed in a mailing envelope, you can enter one ounce as the item weight in your Etsy listing. This will allow you to accurately calculate the shipping cost for your stickers and ensure that you are covering your costs.

It's important to be accurate when specifying the weight of your items, as this can affect the cost of shipping and may impact the appeal of your products to customers. If you understate the weight of your items, you may not be able to cover the cost of shipping and could end up losing money on orders. On the other hand, if you overestimate the weight, your products may appear more expensive to customers and may be less likely to sell.

When a customer purchases two or more items from your Etsy shop, the combined weight of the items will be used to calculate the shipping cost. Etsy will automatically combine the weights of the items when calculating the shipping cost, but the combined weight may be higher than the actual weight of the items.

For example, if a customer purchases five stickers from your shop, the combined weight of the stickers may be higher than the actual weight of the stickers. In this case, you may need to manually adjust the shipping weight when printing out a shipping label to ensure that the correct shipping cost is charged.

Keep in mind that it's important to be accurate when specifying the weight of your items, as this can affect the cost of shipping and may impact the appeal of your products to customers. If you understate the weight of your items, you may not be able to cover the cost of shipping and could end up losing money on orders. On the other hand, if you overestimate the weight, your products may appear more expensive to customers and may be less likely to sell.

Item Size: When setting up your Etsy listings, you'll need to specify the dimensions of the packaging for your stickers. This includes the length, width, and height of the envelope or package that you'll be using to ship the stickers. It's important to be accurate when entering the dimensions of your packaging, as this can affect the cost of shipping.

The dimensions of the package may also impact the appeal of your products to customers, as some shoppers may be interested in the size and appearance of the packaging. For example, if you are using a standard envelope that measures 5x7 inches and has a height less than .25 inches, you can enter the dimensions as 5x7x.25 in the "Item Size" field when setting up your Etsy listing. This will allow you to accurately calculate the shipping cost and ensure that you are covering your costs.

It's a good idea to keep a variety of envelopes or packages on hand to accommodate different sizes and quantities of stickers. This will allow you to select the appropriate packaging for each order and ensure that your stickers are well-protected during shipping. If a customer orders multiple items and I have to use different packaging, I will change the dimensions when I go to ship the order.

Returns and exchanges: When setting up your Etsy listings, you'll have the opportunity to specify your policy on returns and exchanges. This is the policy that you'll follow if a customer is not satisfied with their purchase and wishes to return the item or request an exchange.

It's common for small online sellers, including those who sell stickers on Etsy, to not accept returns or exchanges unless the item arrives damaged or defective. This is because handling returns and exchanges can be time-consuming and costly, and many sellers are unable to afford the resources necessary to do so.

If you decide to allow customers to return items for refunds or exchanges, you can specify your policy in the "Returns and Exchanges" field when setting up your Etsy listings. This will let your customers know what to expect if they are not satisfied with their purchase. Keep in mind that having a clear and straightforward return and exchange policy can help to build trust with your customers and improve the chances of making a sale.

Publish: Congratulations on creating your first Etsy listing! Once you have completed all of the required fields and are satisfied with your listing, you can click the "Publish" button to make it live on Etsy's website.

Before publishing your listing, you may want to preview it to see what it will look like once it's live. To do this, you can click on the "Preview" button. This will allow you to see how your listing will appear to potential customers on Etsy's website.

Once you are satisfied with your listing and have clicked "Publish", it will become live on Etsy's website and available for customers to view and purchase. It's a good idea to regularly review and update your listings to ensure that they are accurate and up to date. This can help to improve the visibility and appeal of your products and increase your chances of making a sale. You can edit or even delete a listing at any time.

Your Second Listing: Creating your second Etsy listing can be much easier if you use the "sell similar" method. This allows you to copy your first listing and simply change out the specific details to create a new listing.

To use the "sell similar" method, you'll need to locate your first listing in your Etsy shop and click the little screw icon in your listing, which will bring up a drop-down menu. Select "Copy Listing,", which will create a new draft listing that is based on your first listing. You can then edit the draft listing to update the details and make any necessary changes.

Using the "sell similar" method can save you time and effort when creating new listings, as you won't need to start from scratch and enter all of same the information again. It's a useful tool for sellers who have multiple similar products, as it allows you to quickly create new listings with minimal effort.

Keep in mind that while the "sell similar" method can be a convenient way to create new listings, it's important to carefully review and update the details of each listing to ensure that they are accurate and correct for the new item you are listing.

Let's say your first listing was for a set of Christmas planner sticker sheets. You now want to list a set of Easter planner sticker sheets. Go to the listing for the Christmas planner sticker sheets and click on the "Copy Listing" option. This will create a new draft listing that is based on your first listing. You can then go through and update the details to reflect the specifics of your new product, such as changing the pictures, title, and description to match the new product, and changing all of the Christmas specifics to Easter.

PRO TIP: List like items in batches so that you can use the "sell similar" trick with each listing needing minimal changes. If you have ten sets of sticker sheets, listing them one after the other means most of the listing fields and the shipping settings will remain the same. You will only need to change certain details. This will help you get your listings up fast, which gives you a better chance of making a sale.

CHAPTER EIGHT: HOW TO SHIP YOUR ETSY STICKER ORDERS

The time has come: You've made your first Etsy sale! Now it's time to ship out the order to your customer. To do this, you will need to follow these steps:

1. Go to the "Shop Manager" and click on the "Orders & Shipping" tab.
2. Under the "New" tab, you will find a list of orders that you need to ship.
3. Click on the order that you want to process.
4. Review the order details to make sure you have all the necessary information, including the shipping address and any special instructions from the customer.
5. If you need to, you can send a message to the customer through Etsy to clarify any details or ask any questions.
6. Print out a shipping label and attach it to the package.

Let's say I have just gotten in an order for a single vinyl sticker. To process it, I log into my Etsy account and go to my "Shop Manager". On the left-hand side of the page, I click on the "Orders & Shipping" tab, which will bring up the page where pending and completed orders are. I click on the "New" tab and all pending orders are listed. I simply click on the box that contains the order, which will bring up a pop-up window where I can purchase a shipping label.

Once you've clicked on the order and the shipping label screen appears, you can select the option to "Get Shipping Labels." This will open a new screen where you can confirm the weight and dimensions of the package. Be sure to double-check these details to ensure that the shipping label you purchase is accurate and appropriate for your package.

Since I have already set up my shipping profile in the listing, the shipping options should be automatically configured to print a First-Class Mail label for a package weighing one ounce. If the dimensions are incorrect for any reason, I can easily edit them. For a single sticker, I already know the weight will be under one ounce when it is placed inside a mailing envelope.

If you sell several items and the combined weight is higher than what you entered for the shipping profile, you can easily change the weight. For example, let's say someone purchases twenty vinyl stickers from me. I would package the stickers and put them in an envelope. I would then weigh the envelope using the digital postal scale I keep next to my desk. The weight comes up to over two ounces. I then change the weight of the order to three ounces. Remember that you need to round up your weights to the next highest number. Etsy will recalculate the shipping cost for the new weight.

After verifying that the weight, dimensions, and postage cost are accurate, you can click the "Review" button to proceed to the review stage. A final screen will appear, allowing you to review the cost of the label before purchasing it. You can then choose to purchase and print the shipping label, using a thermal printer or another printing method. It's important to make sure that the shipping label is printed clearly and accurately so that the package can be properly shipped and delivered to the intended recipient.

Note that if you print a label in error, you can void it and print a new one. The cost of postage is taken directly out of your pending balance; and any labels your void may take a few days to be reimbursed.

Etsy will notify the customer when their package has shipped. There is no need to message your customer directly unless there is an issue with their order.

Packaging Orders: Packing Etsy sticker orders is usually a quick and easy process since stickers are flat and ship in envelopes; they do not need bubble wrap or packing peanuts. After years of shipping vintage collectibles on eBay, I love not having to assemble boxes for Etsy orders!

To ship stickers, you will need the following supplies:

Envelopes: To package orders for my stickers, I use brown craft envelopes with peel-and-stick closures. I have two sizes in stock: 5x7 inches and 6x9 inches, which are suitable for most of my orders. However, if you sell sticker sheets or other larger items, you may need to purchase larger envelopes such as 8.5x11 inches.

There are several places where you can find envelopes for your business:

- **Amazon:** The mega online retailer has a wide selection of envelopes in various sizes and styles, including craft envelopes in various colors and sizes. You can often find good deals and bulk discounts on envelopes from Amazon. They also have the most sizes and styles available.
- **Office supply stores:** Stores like Staples and Office Depot/ OfficeMax carry a variety of envelopes, including craft envelopes, although you likely won't find as many size or color options as compared to Amazon. You can also find envelopes at smaller independent office supply stores.
- **Target, Walmart, and other retail stores:** These stores often carry envelopes in their office supply sections. You may be able to find craft envelopes or other types of envelopes at these stores although selection will vary by location.
- **Michael's:** This arts and crafts store carries a variety of

envelopes, including craft envelopes, in its paper and envelopes section. You may be able to find envelopes at other craft stores as well, but Michael's in particular is well-suited for Etsy sellers looking for shipping supplies.

Clear Bags: Using clear bags can be a good way to add an extra layer of protection for your stickers, especially if you are concerned about the envelope getting wet during shipping. I keep a few different sizes of clear bags on hand so that I have the right size for different orders. However, the 3x5 inch size is my most used bag as my 3" stickers and magnets fit inside perfectly.

As with the mailing envelopes I use, I also use clear bags with self-seal closures, as these make the packaging process more efficient. With self-seal bags, you don't have to worry about using tape or other types of closures to seal the bags. Amazon is a good place to find clear bags, and you may also be able to find them at office supply stores or packaging supply stores.

Printer & Labels: There are a few different options for addressing and posting your Etsy sticker orders, but using a shipping label printer is arguably the most efficient and professional way to print shipping labels. On Etsy, you can purchase and print shipping labels directly from the platform. This will save you time and effort compared to handwriting addresses or taking orders to the post office.

To print shipping labels from Etsy, you'll need a printer that is compatible with the labels you are using. There are two different types of printers that you can use:

Thermal Printer: This type of printer doesn't use ink, but it does require special labels. It's a good option if you want to avoid the hassle of replacing ink cartridges or toner. A thermal printer works by using heat to transfer inkless media onto paper. It consists of a print head with a row of tiny heating elements that are activated according to the digital image of the document being printed. When the heating elements are activated, they cause a thermal reaction in the inkless media, which results in the transfer of the media onto the paper.

I use a Rollo thermal printer specifically for printing my Etsy sticker shop order labels. While I do not have to purchase ink for the printer, I do have to buy special labels.

LaserJet Printer: This type of printer uses toner to print, and it can be a good option for printing shipping labels as well as packing slips for larger orders. LaserJet printers are known for their speed, reliability, and high-quality printing. They can print on a wide range of media, including envelopes, labels, and cardstock. This means you could run envelopes through a LaserJet printer and print the customer's address directly on the envelope, skipping the need for labels altogether.

LaserJet printers are more efficient and cost-effective than inkjet printers when it comes to printing large volumes of documents. However, they do require toner, which can be more expensive than ink in the long run. I use my LaserJet printer to print packing slips for larger Etsy orders.

Enclosures: Including free items in orders is a common practice among Etsy sticker shops. This can be a nice way to show appreciation to your customers and promote your business. There are a couple of different types of free items that you can consider offering in your orders:

- **Stickers or magnets with your URL or brand name:** These can be a good way to promote your business and encourage customers to visit your shop or website. If you print your stickers, you can create these yourself. I use StickerMule to print my enclosure stickers. I have a wide variety of both stickers and magnets with my URL printed on them.

- **Stickers or magnets from your shop:** If you have extra stickers that you didn't list in your shop, you can include these as free items in orders. This could be a good way to clear out your inventory and to provide customers with a surprise bonus.

The number of free items you include in an order can depend on the size of the order. For example, you might include one free item with orders of one or two items, and two or more free items with orders of three or more items. You can also consider offering free items with every order, regardless of the size. Experiment with different approaches and see what works best for your shop.

Seals: Using a sticker to seal your envelopes can be a nice touch for your packaging, as it adds an extra element of design and helps to keep the envelope closed. However, it's not necessary to use a sticker seal on your envelopes, and you may find that it's more efficient to simply use the peel-and-stick closure on the envelope.

If you do decide to use a sticker seal, you can design your own using a graphics program or purchase pre-made sticker seals from a supplier. You can find sticker seals in a variety of shapes, sizes, and styles on Amazon and even Etsy. I created mine on Canva and then had sheets printed on Vistaprint.

Mailing Orders: When I have finished packaging a sticker order, I place it in a bin designated for outgoing orders. I then leave all my orders in my mailbox for the USPS carrier to collect. It is worth noting that while USPS carriers will always collect outgoing envelopes, they may not automatically pick up packages unless they are aware that they are ready for pickup. Therefore, if I have multiple packages, rather than just envelopes, I put in for free USPS carrier pickup.

Note that most USPS mail drop boxes are designed for letters and small flat packages only. If you have outgoing packages that do not fit in the drop box or you do not want to leave them for your carrier, you will need to bring them to the post office yourself. It is also worth noting that some mail drop boxes may have size or weight restrictions, so it is always a good idea to check with the post office or on the USPS website for the specific guidelines for the mail drop box you are using.

PRO TIP: If you have a lot of outgoing Etsy orders for your USPS carrier to collect, and if you are getting numerous packages of supplies to run your shop, consider leaving snacks out for your delivery drivers. I have a box filled with pre-packed candy bars, chips, and cookies that I leave out for those who collect and deliver packages to my home. I buy these snacks in bulk from Sam's Club.

A note about USPS First Class Mail: When you ship stickers via USPS First Class Mail, which is the equivalent of using a stamp, and print the shipping label through Etsy, the package will be assigned a tracking number. Both you and your customer will see the tracking number in your dashboard. The number is a clickable link, which will usually show you where the package is in transit and when it is delivered.

I say usually because USPS First Class Mail tracking isn't as reliable as package or Priority shipments. And sometimes carriers work ahead and scan envelopes as delivered before they actually deliver them to the mailboxes.

If you ship via USPS First Class Mail, you will likely get messages from customers who haven't received their orders even though tracking shows they did. This is typical because the envelope was scanned before the carrier delivered it. When I get messages about undelivered packages, I calmly explain that it is likely the envelope was pre-scanned and will actually be delivered that day or the next. 99.9% of the time, this is the case, and the package ends up being delivered. If the package never shows up, I point the customer to file a claim through Etsy. When tracking shows that an order has been delivered, Etsy will handle the refunding of the order to the customer without it negatively affecting your shop.

CHAPTER NINE: HOW TO ADVERTISE & GROW YOUR STICKER SHOP

When e-commerce was still in its early stages, there were few shopping websites and customers were limited in where they could buy things online. When I began selling online, the only online retailers were eBay and Amazon, and for years I sold on both. Because customers only had these two websites to shop on, I didn't have to compete for shoppers.

However, the e-commerce landscape has changed significantly since I began my online selling career. There are now thousands of online shopping websites available, including Etsy. This increase in competition means that simply listing your stickers for sale is no longer enough to ensure sales. Etsy sellers must actively seek out buyers and take steps to differentiate themselves to attract customers.

To run a successful Etsy sticker shop, you need to engage in promotion and marketing efforts to make your stickers more visible and attract buyers. This can include using the various promotional tools available on the Etsy platform, such as promoted listings and advertising, as well as marketing your stickers on social media platforms and other online channels. By taking these extra steps, you can stand out in a crowded market and attract more buyers to your stickers.

Fortunately, many free and easy-to-use promotional tools can help you increase traffic to your Etsy shop and boost sales. Some of the strategies we'll be discussing in this chapter may require a small investment, such as setting up a website or printing promotional materials, but the potential benefits they can bring to your Etsy shop are worth the price.

Blog/Website: Creating a blog or dedicated website can be a great way to build a stronger connection with your customers and establish your sticker brand. By regularly updating your site with posts about new inventory, you can keep visitors engaged and interested. This can be especially valuable if you plan to make your Etsy shop your primary source of income.

However, it is important to be consistent in maintaining your site and not let it become outdated or neglected. Customers may be turned off by sites that have not been updated in a long period, so be sure to commit to regularly maintaining your site if you decide to create one.

However, if your Etsy sticker shop is only a hobby or part-time job, you may not need to create a dedicated website or blog. Instead, you can focus on promoting your stickers on the Etsy platform and other online channels. If you do decide to create a website, you should consider whether you have the time and resources to maintain it regularly. Some things to consider when deciding whether to create a website include:

- Do you plan to write lengthy articles discussing the items you sell?

- Are you looking to use your site not just as a sales channel but also as a teaching tool? Do you want to sell products only through Etsy or do you plan to sell your stickers on other online sites (such as Amazon, eBay, or Shopify) or at brick-and-mortar retail locations?

- Do you want to explore affiliate advertising or sell advertising on your site to earn extra money?

If you answered "yes" to any of the above questions, then you may want to consider starting a website. However, you will need to decide whether to go with a free blogging platform or a paid website. If you decide to go the paid route, you can invest in a sophisticated system or choose a simple, low-cost one. Yes, there are lots of decisions to make!

There are several free blogging platforms available, such as Blogger and WordPress, that you can use to create a blog for your Etsy shop. It's worth noting that Blogger is owned by Google, which means that you can apply for a Google AdSense account and place ads on your blog to generate additional revenue. In addition to driving traffic to your Etsy listings and increasing sales, a blog can be a useful way to monetize your online presence.

If you decide to create a paid website for your Etsy shop, it's important to do your research and choose a platform that meets your needs. Your Etsy shop should be the focus of your brand, with your blog or website serving as an additional tool to drive traffic to your listings. There are many low-cost website options available, such as GoDaddy.com and Wix.com, which offer not only URL registrations but also inexpensive hosting and simple website-building tools. Keep in mind that your goal is to drive traffic to your Etsy listings and increase sales, so choose a website platform that will help you achieve this.

If you sell your products on multiple websites in addition to Etsy, a blog or website is a great place to provide links to those other platforms, such as Amazon, eBay, Shopify, or brick-and-mortar stores. In addition to posting updates about new inventory and sales, you can also use your blog or website to provide a more personal look into your business and share what's happening behind the scenes. A website can also help to establish your business as legitimate and build trust with potential customers, making them more likely to purchase from you than other sellers.

It's important to remember that maintaining your blog or website is just as important as creating it. In addition to posting regular updates, you should also make an effort to respond to any comments from visitors and ensure that all links are active and up to date.

If you are selling a large number of items on Etsy and plan to continue doing so as your primary business, you may want to consider registering for a domain name, which is a personal website address that is closely tied to your Etsy shop name. This can make it easier for customers to find and remember your website, as well as give you a professional online presence. You can purchase domain names through websites like GoDaddy.com and link them to your Etsy shop or other online platforms. For example, I have the domain "AnnEckhart.com" that directs users directly to my Amazon Storefront where all my books are listed.

As you consider registering for a domain name, it's important to think about where you want the URL to direct users. Do you want people to go to your blog first, or do you want them to always go directly to your Etsy shop? It's important to remember that your blog or website should complement your Etsy shop, rather than serve as a replacement for it.

If you are using a free blog on a platform like Blogger, you may want to choose a domain name that directs people directly to your Etsy shop, such as "MyStore.com", and keep the URL provided by Blogger for your blog as-is. Alternatively, you could choose a different domain name specifically for your blog, such as "MyEtsyShopBlog.com". The key is to choose a URL that makes sense for your business and helps to drive traffic to your Etsy shop.

In my opinion, it's important to have a personalized URL address that points directly to your Etsy shop, as your primary focus should always be on driving sales through Etsy. Your website should work to direct traffic to your Etsy listings, rather than intercept it. If you use the same name for your business on multiple online platforms, such as Amazon and Etsy, you may want to consider registering a domain name that reflects this.

Mailing List: Creating a strong sticker brand can lead to repeat customers who keep coming back to your store because they enjoy your products. To keep these loyal customers informed and engaged, you may want to consider setting up a mailing list. This can be a useful tool for staying in touch with your customers and providing them with updates about your business, such as new product releases, special offers, and other important news. By building a strong relationship with your customers through a mailing list, you can foster customer loyalty and encourage them to continue shopping with you in the future.

Some popular mailing list services include Mailchimp, Constant Contact, AWeber, Campaign Monitor, GetResponse, and Drip. These services provide tools for creating and managing email campaigns, including email design templates, subscriber lists, analytics, and automation features. Many also offer integrations with other marketing and sales tools, such as e-commerce platforms and CRM software.

Note that many blogs and website platforms also have a built-in mailing list feature. For example, I have several websites through GoDaddy, all of which have a feature where visitors can enter their email addresses to join my mailing lists. Collecting email addresses will allow you to send newsletters, promotional emails, or other types of communications to your customers regularly to create brand loyalty and drive shoppers to your Etsy shop.

It's important to ensure that you are only sending emails to individuals who have specifically opted in to receive them, to comply with anti-spam laws, and avoid annoying or alienating your subscribers. By providing valuable and relevant content to your subscribers and respecting their inboxes, you can build a strong and engaged mailing list that can help you drive sales and grow your business.

Facebook: If you want to grow a successful Etsy sticker shop, creating a Facebook page is a valuable marketing tool. Some Etsy sellers opt to use their personal Facebook page as their business page, but I disagree with this approach as you want to keep your personal and business lives separate. A personal Facebook page allows users to add you as a "friend," while a business page requires users to "like" the page to follow it.

By setting up a dedicated business page on Facebook, you can create a professional online presence for your sticker business and reach a wider audience. After all, you can't depend on your friends and family to be your customers; you will need to extend your reach to find customers who not only like your stickers but will buy them.

You can use a Facebook business page to promote your stickers, share updates about your business, and interact with your customers. It is easy to link to your Etsy shop on your Facebook page so that users can easily access your products. By building a following on Facebook and actively engaging with your audience, you can drive traffic to your Etsy shop and increase sales.

To create a Facebook business page, follow these simple steps:

1. Go to facebook.com/about/pages
2. Log in to your personal Facebook account
3. Follow the prompts to create a new business page

Setting up a business page on Facebook is a quick and easy process, and it's completely free. Simply visit the above URL, log in to your personal Facebook account, and the system will guide you through the steps needed to create your business page.

The first decision you will need to make is to name your page. I currently have several Facebook pages, including one for my Etsy Shop.

My Facebook page name is Jean Lee Publishing, which matches my Etsy Shop name.

As you create additional social media accounts related to your Etsy business, it's important to make sure that they all have the same name to establish a cohesive online presence. You will want all your social media account names to match or closely match your Etsy shop name.

There are many ways to personalize your Facebook business page to make it unique and reflective of your brand. Some options include:

1. **Adding a profile picture:** This is the main image that will appear next to your page name and posts. I advise that you use the same profile picture for your Facebook page that you use for your Etsy shop.
2. **Adding a banner:** This is the large image that appears at the top of your Facebook page. You can use a custom banner that you have designed or make on a site like Fiverr.com, or you can create your graphics using tools like Canva or WordSwag. Just as you want your profile picture to be the same across your Etsy shop and all social media accounts, it's also a good idea to make your Facebook banner match or closely match the one in your Etsy shop.
3. **Customizing your page's tabs:** Facebook allows you to add various tabs to your page, such as an events calendar or a shop tab. You can customize these tabs to suit your business and make it easier for users to find the information they are looking for.

It's important to complete the "About" section on your Facebook business page to provide visitors with information about your business. This can include details about your products and services, your business history and mission, and your contact information. However, since this is a business page and separate from your page, it's important to be mindful of the information you share.

For example, while you may want to include your phone number on your page so that friends and family can contact you, it may not be appropriate to include it on your business page unless you have a brick-and-mortar location that you want customers to visit or call. In this case, you may want to consider setting up a separate business phone line or using a contact form on your website or Etsy shop to allow customers to get in touch with you.

Page Category: Several categories may be relevant for an Etsy sticker shop on Facebook. Some options include:

1. **Shopping & Retail:** This category is suitable for businesses that sell physical products, such as stickers, clothing, or home goods.
2. **Arts & Crafts:** This category is suitable for businesses that sell handmade or creative products, such as stickers, jewelry, or paintings.
3. **Gifts & Specialty Items:** This category is suitable for businesses that sell unique or specialty items, such as stickers, gift baskets, or custom products.
4. **Printing & Signage:** This category is suitable for businesses that offer printing or signage services, such as stickers, signs, or custom invitations.

It's important to choose a category that accurately reflects your business and the products you sell. This will help to ensure that your Facebook page is visible to the right audience and that users can easily find and follow your page. You can also add additional categories later if needed, by editing your page's settings.

One way to personalize your Facebook business page is to edit the URL to reflect the name of your page, which is typically the name of your Etsy shop. This can make it easier for users to find and follow your page, as well as establish a cohesive online presence.

To edit the URL of your Facebook business page, follow these steps:

1. Go to your Facebook page and click on the "About" tab.
2. Click on the "Edit" button next to the "Page Info" section.
3. Scroll down to the "Username" field and click on the "Create" button.
4. Enter the desired username and click "Save".

Once you have saved your new username, your Facebook URL will be updated to reflect the name of your page. You can share this URL with customers and promote it on your other social media platforms and online listings to drive traffic to your Facebook page and increase engagement with your brand.

The "About" section of your Facebook page has two description fields: a "Short Description" and a "Long Description." The "Short Description" is a brief overview of your business, while the "Long Description" provides more detailed information.

- Use the "Short Description" to provide a brief overview of your Etsy shop, such as the exact types of stickers you offer, your target audience, and/or your shop's mission. Keep it concise and to the point, using keywords that accurately describe your business.
- Use the "Long Description" to provide more detailed information about your business, such as your history, values, and unique selling points. This is a good place to share your Etsy sticker shop journey, explain why you started your

business, and what your long-term goals are.

In addition to filling out the "About" section of your Facebook business page with information about your Etsy sticker shop, you can also use the "General Information" field to share links to your other social media accounts.

To add links to your other social media accounts, follow these steps:

1. Go to your Facebook page and click on the "About" tab.
2. Click on the "Edit" button next to the "Page Info" section.
3. Scroll down to the "General Information" field and click on the "Add a Website" button.
4. Enter the URL of your social media account and click "Save".

You can add links to as many social media accounts as you like, including Instagram, Twitter, Pinterest, YouTube, and more. It's important to note that you should put the address to your Etsy shop in the main "Website" field, as your primary goal is to drive traffic to your Etsy listings.

One way to make it easy for users to shop your Etsy listings from your Facebook business page is to add a "Shop Now" tab with a call-to-action (CTA) button. This will create a direct link to your Etsy shop, allowing users to easily browse and purchase your products.

To add a "Shop Now" tab to your Facebook business page, follow these steps:

1. Go to your Facebook page and click on the "More" tab at the top of the page.
2. Select "Manage Tabs" from the drop-down menu.
3. Scroll down to the "Add a Tab" section and click on the "Add a Button" button.

4. From the list of options, select "Shop Now" as the type of CTA button you want to add.
5. Enter the URL of your Etsy shop in the "Webpage Link" field and click "Save".

The "Shop Now" tab and CTA button will now appear on your Facebook business page, allowing users to easily access your Etsy listings and make purchases. You can customize the text and appearance of the CTA button to match your branding and create a cohesive look and feel for your page.

The "Settings" tab on your Facebook business page allows you to control how users can interact with you and your page. This can be particularly useful if you have stringent privacy settings or want to limit the types of interactions you receive.

To access the Settings tab, follow these steps:

1. Go to your Facebook page and click on the "Settings" tab at the top of the page.
2. From the left-hand menu, select "Messages" to manage your messaging preferences.
3. Under the "General" section, you can choose to allow or block users from messaging you and whether or not you want to receive notifications when you receive a new message.
4. You can also choose to allow or block users from posting on your page and whether or not you want to receive notifications when you receive a new post.
5. Scroll down to the "Blocking" section to block specific users or groups from interacting with your page. By adjusting the settings on your Facebook business page, you can control how users can interact with you and manage the types of interactions you receive. Keep in mind that you can always

change these settings later if your preferences change.

Once you have set up your Facebook business page, it's important to start building your audience by getting people to "like" your page. One way to do this is to invite friends and family to your page to "like" your new business page. This can help to get the word out about your business and start building a following. However, remember that you can't expect your friends and family to buy from you or even "like" your page.

In addition to inviting friends and family to "like" your page, you can also include the link to your Facebook page on any package enclosures that you send out. For example, you can include a business card-sized "thank you" note in each order that includes the direct link to your Etsy shop as well as the links to your blog and social media accounts.

You can also use Facebook Ads to target specific groups of people who may be interested in your products and encourage them to "like" your page.

To create a Facebook ad:

1. Go to your Facebook business page and click on the "Create" button at the top of the page.
2. From the drop-down menu, select "Ad" to create a new ad campaign.
3. Choose your ad objective. Facebook offers a range of ad objectives to choose from, including "Website Visits," "Conversions," "Product Catalog Sales," and more. Select the one that best fits your business goals.
4. Set up your targeting options. Facebook allows you to target specific groups of people based on demographics, interests, behaviors, and more. Use the targeting options to narrow down your audience to the people most likely to be interested

in your products.

5. Select your ad placements. You can choose to show your ad on Facebook, Instagram, or both, as well as on other platforms such as Audience Network and Marketplace.

6. Set your budget and schedule. Decide how much you want to spend on your ad campaign and over what period. You can choose to run your ad continuously or set specific start and end dates.

7. Create your ad. Use the ad creation tools to design your ad, including the ad format, images, text, and call-to-action (CTA) button. You can choose from a variety of ad formats, including single images, carousels, and videos.

8. Review and submit your ad. Once you have finished creating your ad, review all the details to make sure everything is correct. When you are ready, click "Submit" to create your ad campaign.

The "Boost Post" feature on Facebook is a paid advertising tool that allows you to promote a specific post from your Facebook business page to a larger audience. This can help to increase the reach and visibility of your post, which can lead to more engagement and ultimately more sales for your Etsy sticker shop.

To boost a post from your Facebook business page, follow these steps:

1. Go to your Facebook business page and find the post that you want to promote.

2. Click on the "Boost Post" button below the post.

3. Select your target audience. You can choose to show your boosted post to people who already like your page, to a specific group of people based on demographics and interests, or to a custom audience that you define.

4. Set your budget and duration. Decide how much you want to

spend on your boosted post and over what period. You can choose to boost your post for as little as $1 per day or as much as you want.

5. Review and boost your post. Once you have finished setting up your boosted post, review all the details to make sure everything is correct. When you are ready, click "Boost" to promote your post.

So, you have set up a Facebook page for your business and have started getting people to "Like" it. Now what? Providing helpful content on your page will be vital to keeping it up to date and attracting new followers.

I share my newest listings directly to my Facebook page, as Etsy makes this incredibly easy to do.

To share an Etsy listing on your Facebook page, follow these steps:

1. Go to your Etsy shop and find the listing that you want to share.
2. Click on the "Share" button below the listing.
3. Select "Facebook" from the drop-down menu.
4. A pop-up window will appear, asking you to log in to your Facebook account. Enter your login credentials and click "Log In.
5. A new window will appear, allowing you to customize the message that will be posted to your Facebook page along with the listing. You can add a message or simply leave the default message. 6. When you are ready, click "Post to Facebook" to share the listing on your Facebook page.

In addition to promoting your listings on social media, it's a good idea to engage with your followers and keep them informed about your business. You can do this by posting updates about new inventory, sales, or other relevant information on your business page. Creating polls about new product ideas is another good way to create engagement. Note that when people engage with your Facebook posts, Facebook may show the engagement in that person's feed so that their friends can see it. And those friends, seeing that they know someone who follows your page, may decide to follow your page, too.

It's important to keep your posts positive and avoid posting about controversial or offensive topics. In other words, unless you are selling religious or political stickers, steer clear of those two topics. The goal of your business page is to attract customers and make money. Posting about sensitive subjects can potentially turn people away. It's better to stick to topics related to your business and save the personal commentary for your personal page.

Twitter: Twitter is another popular social media platform that can be useful for promoting your sticker business. With Twitter, you can share short updates, called "tweets," with your followers and engage with them through @replies and hashtags. Twitter is a fast-paced and dynamic platform, and it's a good way to share quick updates and engage with your audience in real-time.

If you don't already have a Twitter account, you can create one for free at Twitter.com. Alternatively, if you have an existing personal account that you are active on, you may want to consider creating a separate account for your Etsy business to keep your personal and professional lives separate. It's a good idea to use the same handle for your Twitter account, Etsy shop, and Facebook business page to create a consistent online presence for your business. This will make it easier for people to find and follow you across different platforms.

Twitter limits their "tweets" to 280 characters or less. Etsy makes it easy to share your listings on Twitter by including a share button in all active listings. To use the Twitter share button, simply click on it within a listing, and a new window will open on Twitter with the title of your listing and the direct link to it already populated. You can send the "tweet" as is or customize the message as well as add hashtags.

Hashtags (marked as such with the # sign) are a way to categorize and organize content on social media platforms, especially on Twitter. In fact, I find that hashtags are more useful on Twitter than on any other platform. Users can follow their favorite hashtags to keep up with the posts they are most interested in seeing.

Adding hashtags to your "tweets" can be an effective way to increase the visibility of your posts and reach people who are buying stickers. By adding relevant hashtags to your tweets, you can make it easier for people to discover your Etsy business and perhaps buy your stickers.

To use hashtags effectively, it's important to choose hashtags that are relevant to your sticker business and the content you are sharing. For example, let's say you have a set of unicorn-themed planner stickers. When you click on the Twitter icon in the listing, your title and the link to the listing will automatically populate to Twitter. If there is room to add more text, you may consider adding hashtags such as #plannerstickers, #stickers, #unicorns, #etsystickershop, and/or #plannercommunity. These hashtags will help your tweet show up in searches for these topics, meaning they will show up for Twitter users following those hashtags.

It's worth noting that it's important not to overuse hashtags or use ones that are not relevant to your business. This can make your tweets seem spammy and could turn people off. Instead, choose a few relevant hashtags that accurately describe your business and the stickers you are selling. This will help you reach the right audience and increase the chances that your tweets will be seen and that users may click through to your Etsy shop.

It's a good idea to share your Twitter handle with your customers, both online and offline, to encourage them to follow you on the platform. There are a few ways you can do this:

1. Include your Twitter handle in your online profiles, such as your blog or website, as well as on other social media platforms and online directories.
2. Share your Twitter handle in your email signature and on business cards or other promotional materials.
3. Encourage your customers to follow you on Twitter by including a call to action in your emails, newsletters, or other communications.

One way to build up your followers on Twitter is to follow other users and engage with their content. Some users follow everyone who follows them, which can help increase your follower count. You can also use Twitter's @reply and retweet features to engage with other users and share their content with your followers. This can help build relationships and expose your content to a wider audience.

PRO TIP: Connect with other Etsy sellers on Twitter. However, avoid connecting with other sticker shops (unless they sell completely different stickers than you do) as this creates unnecessary jealousy and competition. Instead, search the hashtag #etsyshop and follow users whose products you like. Most Etsy sellers love to connect with shops that aren't in direct competition with their own. Promote their shops by retweeting their posts and they may do the same in return, which will help you attract new customers.

Just like on Facebook, you can use Twitter to send and receive messages from other users. On Twitter, these messages are called "Direct Messages" or "DMs" for short. You can send DMs to any user who is following you, and you can also receive DMs from users who you follow.

In addition to messaging, Twitter also allows you to create "Lists" to group users you follow into categories. Lists are a useful way to organize and keep track of the accounts you follow, and they can also be used to create customized feeds of tweets from specific users. For example, you might create a list of "customers," "Etsy shops," "stickers," or "planners" to help you stay organized and focused on the content that is most relevant to your business.

Pinterest: Pinterest is a social media platform that allows users to share and discover ideas and inspiration by "pinning" images and videos to virtual boards. As with Facebook and Twitter, Etsy includes a share button in all active listings that makes it easy to share your listings on Pinterest. By sharing your Etsy sticker listings on Pinterest, you can increase the visibility of your products and potentially drive traffic to your shop.

You can share your listings on specific boards that you have created, such as a "Stickers" board, and you can also include relevant hashtags to make it easier for people to discover your content. In addition to sharing your listings on Pinterest, you can also encourage your followers to share your pins with their followers by "repining" them to their boards. This can help expose your content to a wider audience and potentially lead to more clicks and sales.

It can be a concern for Etsy sellers that once an item has sold, the "pin" on Pinterest is no longer relevant. Some sellers choose to delete old pins of items that have sold to keep their boards up to date, while others leave them active. There are pros and cons to both approaches. On one hand, deleting old pins can help keep your boards organized and focused on current products. However, leaving old pins active can have some benefits as well. For example, as you mentioned, someone who sees an old pin of a sold item may still be interested in your business and click through to your Etsy shop or current listings.

If you do become active on Pinterest, be sure to share your Pinterest account with your customers and followers on other social media platforms. There are a few ways you can do this:

1. Include your Pinterest URL on your blog or website, if you have one, and in the "General Information section" of your Facebook page.
2. Share your Pinterest link in your email signature and on business cards or other promotional materials.
3. Periodically share your Pinterest link on Facebook and Twitter to attract new followers and encourage existing followers to visit your Pinterest account.

Instagram: Instagram is a social media platform that allows users to share photos and videos and engage with their followers. There are several features on Instagram that you can use to share your content:

- **Instagram Posts:** Instagram Posts are photos or videos that you share on your profile. They are visible to all your followers and remain on your profile indefinitely unless you delete them. Instagram Posts are a good way to share high-quality images and videos that represent your business and showcase your products.
- **Instagram Stories:** Instagram Stories are photos or videos that you share on your profile that disappear after 24 hours. Instagram Stories are a good way to share ephemeral content, such as behind-the-scenes glimpses of your business, sneak peeks of new products, or other engaging content that you want to share with your followers but that you don't want to remain on your profile indefinitely.

- **Instagram Reels:** Instagram Reels is a feature that allows users to create and share short video clips of up to one minute and thirty seconds that can be edited with music, effects, and other creative tools. Instagram Reels is a good way to create and share fun, creative content that engagingly showcases your products or business.

In addition to using Instagram to promote your Etsy listings, you can also use the platform to connect with your customers on a more personal level by sharing photos that may not always relate directly to your business. This can help you build a stronger connection with your audience and give them a more well-rounded view of your business. To achieve this, you can share photos of your office, packages you are shipping out, and other behind-the-scenes glimpses of your sticker shop.

You can also share photos of your pets, meals, or other personal interests to give your followers a more personal look at your life. It's important to keep in mind, however, that you are using Instagram to promote your Etsy sticker shop. Just as with your other social media business pages, you should avoid sharing controversial or offensive content. I

Just as you use hashtags on Twitter, they are also a useful tool on Instagram. Here are a few tips for using hashtags effectively on Instagram:

1. **Use relevant hashtags:** Make sure to use hashtags that are relevant to your business and the content you are sharing. This will help ensure that your posts are seen by users who are interested in what you are selling. As an Etsy sticker shop, stick to hashtags related to stickers and specifically to the products you are posting about. Many people will use

hashtags that have nothing to do with their Etsy shop to be seen by more users. But this can backfire if those users are annoyed seeing your content in their feed and react negatively by leaving mean comments under your posts.

2. **Use a mix of popular and niche hashtags:** Using popular hashtags can help increase the visibility of your content but using too many popular hashtags can make it harder for your content to stand out. Consider using a mix of popular and niche hashtags to balance visibility and relevance. For example, you will likely use the hashtags #etsy, #etsyshop, and #stickers in most of your Instagram posts. But also add hashtags of the theme of the stickers you are posting about. If you are sharing about your listings of floral stickers, use hashtags such as #flowers, #boho, and "botanical" to reach people who follow those specific tags.

3. **Don't overdo it:** Using too many hashtags can make your content look spammy and may turn off some users. Aim to use around five to seven hashtags per post to strike a good balance between visibility and relevance. A tip is to create a list of hashtags in the notes or memo section of your smartphone that you can simply copy, paste, and edit when you are creating a new post.

Some popular hashtags for Etsy stickers shops include:

- #stickers
- #plannerstickers
- #stickeraddict
- #stickerlove
- #stickerobsession
- #plannergoodies
- #planneraccessories
- #stationeryaddict

- #stickershop
- #stickerobsessed
- #plannercommunity
- #plannergirl
- #stickerart
- #stickerdesign
- #plannerstickeraddict

You cannot link to your Etsy shop in static Instagram posts. However, Instagram allows you to include one website link in your profile, which you can use to link to your Etsy shop. To promote your Etsy listings on Instagram, you can share photos and include a message in the caption that directs your followers to your profile page, where they can find an active link to your Etsy shop. For example, you can write "25% off sale going on right now in our Etsy shop! Follow the link in our profile @yourinstagramaccount to shop now!" By including the @ symbol and your Instagram handle, you can create a clickable link that will take users to your profile page, where they can click on the link to your Etsy shop and browse your listings.

While you can't create a direct link to your Etsy shop in static Instagram posts, you can create a link to your shop when you post an Instagram Story. When you are posting a photo or a video to your Instagram Story, simply click on the little smiley face post-it note on the screen. Several options to customize your Story will come up, including a "LINK" option. Note that you can get a direct link to specific Etsy listings when you are using the Etsy app. You simply copy the Etsy link and paste it into the Instagram Story link to take users straight to the listing.

If you want to share multiple links on Instagram, you will need to use a service like Linktr.ee to create a landing page that allows you to list all your links in one place. When you create a Linktr.ee page, you can add as many links as you like, and users will be able to access them all by clicking on the main Linktr.ee link in your Instagram profile. To see an example, visit my Linktr.ee page at linktr.ee/anneckhart.

TikTok: TikTok is a social media platform that allows users to create and share short, lip-sync, and comedy videos. TikTok began with a younger demographic but is slowly growing with users of all ages. On TikTok, users can create short videos (up to three minutes) that can be edited with music, effects, and other creative tools. From comedy skits and dances to personal stories and business, there are TikTok videos for every interest.

While TikTok may not be as widely used for business purposes as platforms like Facebook, Twitter, and Instagram, it can still be a useful tool for promoting your Etsy shop and building a following. Some businesses have used TikTok exclusively to grow their brands and have gone from struggling start-ups to full-scale companies.

There are two types of TikTok accounts users can create: personal or business. A TikTok personal account is a type of account that is used by individuals for personal use, such as sharing content with friends and family, connecting with others with similar interests, and expressing their creativity. Personal accounts on TikTok do not have access to certain features and tools that are available to business accounts, such as analytics, advertising, and the ability to create and manage ads.

A TikTok business account is a type of account that is specifically designed for businesses to use on the platform. Business accounts on TikTok have access to features and tools that are not available to personal accounts, such as analytics, advertising, and the ability to create and manage ads. The biggest benefit of a TikTok business account is that you can put a clickable URL in your profile. I have my Linktr.ee link in my TikTok business account profile, which will take people to a static page with all of my business links, including a link to my Etsy sticker shop.

If you are an Etsy sticker shop owner and you want to use TikTok to promote your business, you definitely want to create a TikTok business account. Note that you can create multiple TikTok pages within one account; so if you already have a personal account, you can easily add a second business account.

To create a TikTok business account for an Etsy sticker shop, you will need to follow these steps:

1. Download the TikTok app on your phone or tablet.
2. Open the app and tap on the "Me" icon in the bottom right corner.
3. Tap on the three dots in the top right corner and select "Manage account."
4. Tap on "Switch to Professional Account."
5. Select "Business" as the account type.
6. Follow the prompts to complete the account setup process, including adding your business name, contact information, and any other required information.
7. Once your account is set up, you can start creating and sharing content to promote your Etsy sticker shop. Keep in mind that TikTok may require you to verify your business account before you can access all the features and tools available to business accounts. This may involve providing additional information or documentation to prove that you are the owner of the business.

There are several ways you can use TikTok to promote your Etsy sticker shop:

Create and share posts about your products: Use TikTok's creative tools and features, such as music, effects, and filters, to create short, entertaining videos that showcase your products creatively and engagingly. I like to share short videos of new stickers as well as videos of me packing up Etsy orders.

Use relevant hashtags and tags: By including relevant hashtags and tags in your TikTok posts, you can make it easier for users to discover your content and interact with your account as well as hopefully visit your Etsy shop.

Here are some popular TikTok hashtags for Etsy sticker shops:

- #stickers
- #stickeraddict
- #stickerlove
- #stickerobsessed
- #stickerhoarder
- #stickerart
- #stickerdesign
- #stickercollection
- #stickersale
- #stickerartist
- #stickerbusiness
- #stickerbrand

You can also try searching for hashtags related to specific themes or categories, such as #plannerstickers or #vinylstickers. Additionally, you can use TikTok's search function to discover more hashtags related to your specific stickers. Remember to use relevant hashtags when posting about your stickers to help them reach a wider audience.

As I mentioned in the Instagram section of this chapter, I keep a list of hashtags in the notes section of my phone that I just copy and paste into posts.

Collaborate with other users: Collaborating with other users on TikTok can be a great way to promote your business and reach a wider audience. You can partner with other users who have and create content together, or you can participate in TikTok challenges or trends that are related to your business or products. However, you don't want to seek out collaborations with Etsy sticker shops that sell the same products as you. You can also reach out to users with an offer of free stickers if they show your products in a video. While large creators charge for this type of collaboration, smaller accounts may do it for free, your only cost being that you send them stickers to review.

Utilize TikTok's advertising features: TikTok's business accounts have access to advertising features that can help you reach a wider audience beyond those who follow your account and drive traffic to your Etsy shop. You can create and manage ads on TikTok to reach users who are interested in your products or related topics. TikTok's advertising opportunities include:

- **In-feed ads:** These are native ads that appear in users' feeds, like sponsored posts on other social media platforms. They can be in the form of videos, photos, or carousels and can include a call-to-action button.
- **Brand takeover ads:** These are full-screen ads that appear when a user opens the app. They can be in the form of a video or image and are a great way to grab users' attention.
- **Branded hashtag challenge:** This feature allows businesses to create a hashtag challenge, which encourages users to create and share content using the designated hashtag.
- **Branded effects:** TikTok's AR effects allow businesses to

create their own branded filters and lenses that users can use in their videos.

- **Branded hashtag stickers:** These are branded stickers that users can use in their videos and are associated with a specific hashtag.

To access TikTok's advertising platform, you will need to sign up for a TikTok Ads account. Here's how you can do that:

1. Go to the TikTok Ads website at tiktok.com/business/ad-center.
2. Click on the "Sign Up" button in the top right corner of the page.
3. Fill in the required information to create a new account, including your name, email address, and password.
4. Click on the "Sign Up" button to create your account.

Once you have created your account, you can access TikTok's advertising platform by logging in to the TikTok Ads website and clicking on the "Create" button in the top right corner of the page. From there, you can choose the type of ad you want to create and follow the prompts to set up your campaign.

It's worth noting that you may need to verify your account before you can start creating ads on TikTok. This may involve providing additional information or documents to confirm your identity and business information.

YouTube: If you're feeling overwhelmed by all the different social networking sites and techniques, it's important to take things one step at a time. Start with setting up a blog or website, and then move on to Facebook, Twitter, Pinterest, Instagram, and TikTok. Or just choose one to focus on, the one you most enjoy. Some Etsy shops only use Facebook, while others are solely focused on TikTok.

Don't worry about mastering all of the social media platforms at once - focus on getting the hang of one site before moving on to the next. As you become more comfortable with each platform, you can gradually expand your social media presence and use these tools to promote your Etsy shop effectively. Just remember to take deep breaths and relax - there's no need to rush or feel overwhelmed. Rome wasn't built in a day, and neither were the top Etsy shops!

In addition to the main social media platforms discussed earlier, you can also use YouTube to promote your Etsy shop and drive traffic to your listings. YouTube allows you to create and share videos that showcase your products and engage with your audience. You can also monetize your videos through Google's AdSense program, which allows you to earn money from ads that are shown during your videos.

There are many types of YouTube videos you can create to promote your Etsy sticker shop. Here are a few ideas:

Product demos and reviews: Create videos that demonstrate how your stickers can be used and try to sell viewers on the high quality and unique design of your products. Viewers love to see products up close in videos, and videos can be much more effective in selling products than photos.

Behind-the-scenes content: Share a glimpse into the process of creating your stickers, including your design process, printing methods, and packaging. This can help your audience feel more connected to your business and understand the effort that goes into creating your products. A popular TikTok trend is for sellers to film themselves packing up orders using the hashtag #packanorderwithme.

Creative ideas and inspiration: If you have a planner sticker shop, share creative ideas for using your stickers, such as bullet journal spreads, planner layouts, or scrapbook pages. If you sell vinyl stickers, show your followers how they can mix and match different sticker designs to create unique looks on water bottles and laptops.

Collaborations and challenges: Collaborate with other creators or participate in challenges related to stickers and crafting. Find other Etsy sellers who aren't in the sticker category but whose products and designs align with yours. An easy example would be to find another Etsy seller and exchange a surprise box of your products that you can each open on your channels. This will help both of you reach an audience who is already shopping on Etsy but hasn't yet discovered your shops.

Vlogs: Vlogging a day or week in the life of you running your sticker shop is a fun, casual way to connect with potential customers. I have a vlog channel where I film non-business content, but I will occasionally show my stickers in those videos as a way to drive traffic to my Etsy shop.

For more information about utilizing videos to grow your Etsy shop, check out my book *Beginner's Guide To Starting A YouTube Channel,* which you can find on Amazon.

LinkedIn: LinkedIn is a professional networking site that can be a useful tool for promoting your Etsy shop and connecting with potential customers and partners.

Here are some ways you can use LinkedIn to promote your Etsy shop:

1. **Create a company page:** LinkedIn allows businesses to create company pages that showcase their products and services. This can be a great way to introduce your Etsy shop

to LinkedIn users and provide information about your products and business.

2. **Share updates and content:** Use LinkedIn to share updates about your Etsy shop, including new product releases, sales and promotions, and behind-the-scenes content. You can also share relevant articles, blog posts, and other content that showcases your products and expertise.

3. **Connect with others:** LinkedIn is a great place to connect with other professionals, including potential customers and partners. Join relevant groups, participate in discussions, and make connections with others in your industry to expand your network and promote your Etsy shop.

4. **Utilize LinkedIn's advertising features:** LinkedIn offers a range of advertising options that can help you reach a targeted audience and drive traffic to your Etsy shop. These options include sponsored content, sponsored InMail, and display ads.

Putting It All Together: When you have an Etsy shop, your primary concern should be developing new products, creating listings, answering customer questions, and shipping out orders. A good title, photos, and description are crucial to creating an Etsy listing that will result in consistent sales. Think of social media as a bonus step in that listing creation process.

To promote your listings on social media, you can use the "share" buttons provided by Etsy in every active listing. Simply click on the buttons for Facebook, Twitter, and Pinterest to share your listings on these platforms. You can also add hashtags to increase the visibility of your listings. Once you have connected your Etsy account to your social media networks, you can easily share your listings with just a few clicks.

To avoid overwhelming your followers on Facebook with multiple listings at once, it is a good idea to share them individually over some time rather than all at once. This will help ensure that your followers see your posts and are more likely to click through to your listings. On Twitter and Pinterest, it is generally okay to share a larger batch of items at once, as these platforms do not have the same restrictions on business page posts. However, it is still a good idea to spread out your posts and mix in other types of content to keep your followers engaged.

To promote your business on Instagram, it is important to post regularly and engage with other users. Try to post at least a few times a week, if not daily. You can share photos of your office, new inventory, or even personal moments to give your followers a behind-the-scenes look at your business. Don't forget to include three to five hashtags with each post to make it easier for users to find you. And be sure to engage with other users by following them and liking their content. Spend a few minutes each day scrolling through your feed to connect with other users and discover new content. By posting regularly and engaging with your followers, you can build a loyal following and drive traffic to your Etsy shop.

If you have the time and resources to create and maintain a blog or website or produce YouTube videos, these can be great ways to promote your Etsy shop. However, keep in mind that they will require additional work and resources, so it's important to make sure they are worth the investment. If you do decide to use a blog or website or create YouTube content, be sure to share it on your other social media accounts to get the most exposure. This can help drive traffic to your Etsy shop and increase sales. Just be sure to manage your time effectively and prioritize your efforts so that you can get the most benefit from your efforts.

While I put in a lot of effort to market my Etsy shop online, I also have promotional tools I use offline. As I mentioned earlier, I include a packing slip in all my Etsy orders (you can print these directly from Etsy after your shipping label has been printed); and I also include branded stickers that I order from StickerMule. The stickers contain my Etsy shop URL hoping customers will come back to shop with me. It also gives orders a personal touch that helps cultivate positive feedback.

PRO TIP: A great way to create one social media post that you can share across multiple platforms is to first film a TikTok video that is no longer than a minute and a half. You can then share that video on Instagram as a Reel. You can then share the Reel to your Instagram Story and Facebook, as well as upload the video to YouTube as a Short. If you are monetized on YouTube, you can share the link to the YouTube Short to Twitter, as views on the video will translate into Google AdSense income. This method gives you posts across all of the top social media platforms, and you only had to film ONE short video!

Etsy's Marketing Tools: While social media is a great way to build your sticker brand and stop, Etsy itself offers several marketing tools to help sellers promote their products and reach potential customers.

Some of the marketing tools available on Etsy include:

Shop Announcements: This feature allows you to create a message that will be displayed on your shop's homepage and in the emails you send to your customers. You can use this feature to announce sales, new products, or other important updates about your shop. Here are some ways you can utilize this feature to promote your sticker shop:

1. **Share new product releases:** Use your shop announcements to let your customers know about new sticker designs or collections that you have released. You can include photos and details about the stickers, as well as any special

promotions or discounts you are offering.

2. **Highlight popular products:** If you have any stickers that are particularly popular or are selling well, consider using your shop announcements to give them some extra visibility. You can include photos and details about the stickers and why they are so popular.

3. **Share your story:** Use your shop announcements to give your customers a behind-the-scenes look at your business and share your story. You can talk about your inspiration for your stickers, your creative process, or anything else that you think would be of interest to your customers.

4. **Offer promotions and discounts:** Use your shop announcements to offer promotions or discounts to your customers. This can be a great way to drive sales and encourage customers to purchase from your shop.

5. **Keep your customers informed:** Use your shop announcements to keep your customers informed about any changes or updates to your shop, such as new policies or shipping times. This can help build trust and improve customer satisfaction.

Shop Blog: This feature allows you to create a blog within your Etsy shop where you can share news, updates, and other information about your products and business. You can use the same ideas as noted in the "Shop Announcements" section in the blog area.

Etsy Ads: This feature allows you to create targeted ads that will be displayed to potential customers who are searching for products like yours on Etsy. You can set a budget and target specific keywords, categories, and locations to reach the right audience.

To create an ad for your sticker shop on Etsy, you will need to have a seller account and be a part of the Etsy Ads program. Here's how you can create an ad for your sticker shop:

1. Go to the "Promote" tab in your Etsy shop's dashboard.
2. Click on the "Create a new ad" button.
3. Select the type of ad you want to create: you can choose from a promoted listing ad, which will promote a specific listing in your shop, or a shopper ad, which will promote your entire shop.
4. Select the listing or listings you want to promote or choose to promote your entire shop.
5. Set your budget and bid amount. You can choose a daily budget or a lifetime budget, and you can set the maximum bid amount that you are willing to pay per click or impression.
6. Choose your target audience. You can target your ad to specific locations, age ranges, genders, and interests.
7. Create your ad creative. You can use one of your existing listings or create a new ad from scratch. You can add images, text, and a call to action to your ad.
8. Preview your ad and make any necessary adjustments.
9. Click "Submit" to create your ad.

Etsy Offsite Ads: This feature allows you to place ads that will be displayed on other websites and platforms, such as Facebook, Instagram, and Pinterest. For sellers with less than $10,000 in the yearly sale, Etsy offsite ads are an optional program one needs to opt into. However, it is mandatory and automatic for shops that sell over $10,000 a year. You only pay for an offsite ad if it leads to a sale. You do not pay if someone clicks on the ad but does not make a purchase.

You can end your offsite ads at any time unless you are automatically enrolled due to selling over $10,000 a year. There is no way to end or opt out of offsite ads for those sellers. While this may seem unfair, to be honest, if you are selling over $10,000 a year on Etsy, offsite ads should be affordable for you. Again, you only pay if the click on an ad leads to a sale.

The Offsite Ads section is located under the "Settings" tab in your Shop Manager.

Etsy Teams: Etsy teams are groups of Etsy sellers who come together to support each other, share knowledge and resources, and collaborate on projects. There are teams for sellers in specific niches, such as handmade jewelry or vintage clothing, as well as teams for sellers in specific regions or with specific interests.

If you have a sticker shop on Etsy and want to join a team, you can search for teams that might be relevant to your shop. For example, you could join a team for digital product sellers or a team for sticker makers. You can also create your team if you don't find an existing team that meets your needs.

Joining an Etsy team can be beneficial for your sticker shop in several ways:

- You can get feedback and advice from other sellers who have experience in the same or a similar niche.
- You can learn about new trends and techniques that might help you improve your shop.
- You can participate in team promotions and events that can help you reach a wider audience.
- You can collaborate with other sellers on projects, such as cross-promotions or product bundles.

To join an Etsy team, go to the team's page on the Etsy website and click on the "Join Team" button. You may need to answer a few questions or provide some information about your shop before you can join. Once you're a member of a team, you can participate in the team's discussions and activities through the Etsy website or the team's social media channels.

Free Shipping Guarantee: If you are charging customers for shipping, you can opt into Etsy's "Free Shipping Guarantee", which is where customers get free shipping on orders of $35 or more. Etsy will show customers that they can get free shipping in your shop when they order $35, which can help increase your average sale order total.

Most successful Etsy sticker shops offer "free" shipping on all orders, with the cost of postage built into the price of the stickers. However, if you are uncomfortable with offering "free" shipping on smaller orders, the $35 "Free Shipping Guarantee" is a great program to try out. After all, if you are getting a $35 sticker order, you are likely making a nice profit. Therefore, the added cost of postage shouldn't affect you too much.

If you are charging for shipping, Etsy will frequently prompt you to consider their Free Shipping Guarantee. Otherwise, you can find it under "Shipping settings," which is located in the "Settings" section of your seller dashboard.

Sales & Discounts: You can create various sales and discounts for both new and returning customers. You will find the "Sales & Discounts" section under the "Marketing" tab in your Etsy dashboard. You can offer several types of discounts, including:

- **Percentage off:** You can offer a percentage off the purchase price for a specific product or the entire order. For example, you could offer a 10% discount on all stickers in your shop, or a 20% discount on orders over $50.

- **Amount off:** You can offer a fixed amount off the purchase price for a specific product or the entire order. For example, you could offer a $5 discount on all t-shirts in your shop or a $10 discount on orders over $100.
- **Free shipping:** You can offer free shipping on a specific product or for the entire order. This can be a good way to encourage more sales and reduce cart abandonment.
- **Sale events:** You can create a sale event by offering a discount on a selection of your products for a limited time.

Some of the offers you can send include:

- **Thank you:** Invite up to 200 recent customers back with a thank you offer by sending them an offer to show appreciation and encourage them to shop again. You can choose a discount amount of a percentage off, a fixed amount off, or free shipping with an order minimum.
- **Favorited item:** Turn favorites into orders by sending offers to anyone who favors one of your items. You can choose a discount percentage or a fixed amount off. Note that there is no minimum order option for the "favorited item" offers; it applies to a single item that someone has put into their cart.
- **Abandoned cart:** Remind shoppers to check out by sending an offer when someone leaves an item from your shop in their cart. As with "favorited item," you can choose a discount percentage or a fixed amount off; and there is no minimum order amount as the offer applies to a single item that someone has put into their cart.
- **Run a sale:** Set lower prices for your whole shop or select categories. Many professional Etsy sellers will tell you that you should always be running sales and that your sales should be short-term for no longer than 48 hours. This is because

Etsy will show shoppers a countdown clock of the remaining time in a sale, which can create a sense of urgency. These sellers typically run the same sale every two days.

Create a promo code: Etsy allows shops to create a custom code to send to customers directly. You will need to enter a code name, a description of the offer, and the discount amount. You can also choose to set an expiration date and a minimum purchase amount. You can manually end your coupon codes at any time.

Etsy does not distribute these coupon codes; that is something you need to do. If you have a mailing list or Facebook group, you can share special promo codes with them. I have a Facebook group specifically for my Etsy sticker shop and frequently share special promo codes just for them.

To Recap: A website, social media pages, branding, sales, ads, sales, discounts, enclosures, and collaborations. There are so many options available to you as an Etsy seller to market your stickers. And it does require you to invest time, most of these marketing options are free. While it can all seem overwhelming, trust me that promoting your Etsy shop becomes second nature after a while. The increase in sales will make all your extra time and effort worth it in the end!

CHAPTER TEN: HOW TO MANAGE CUSTOMER SERVICE ISSUES

Handling customer service issues is part of owning a business, whether it is online or off. The fact is that no matter how hard you try, you can never please all the people all of the time. Eventually, you will likely have a customer complain about an order.

When it comes to handling customer service issues on Etsy, the first step is to avoid them in the first place. You can do this by ensuring your listings are accurate. Clear photos, thorough descriptions, and clear shop policies all go a long way toward keeping customers happy. Also, shipping orders promptly will help stop customers from asking when you are shipping and when their orders will arrive. I almost always ship orders the following business day.

However, mistakes do happen. Occasionally you may ship the wrong item. If a customer contacts you to let you know you sent them the wrong item, you can do one of two things:

1. Pay for the customer to return the item and ship them the correct one.
2. Refund them completely and let them keep the incorrect item.

I use the second option as it's a hassle for a customer to have to repack and return a package, even though Etsy allows you to send them a return label. I would then have to package and ship a new order once the wrong one arrived back to me. Between paying for the return postage, paying for the new item, and paying for shipping, I would lose a lot of money versus if I just refunded the customer outright and told them to keep the item. Often the customer will reorder the correct item once their refund is processed.

Issuing a Refund: When dealing with upset customers, remain professional, even if someone is attacking you. Offer your apologies and see if you can fix the issue. If you need to issue a refund to the customer, follow these steps:

1. Sign in to your Etsy account and go to your "Orders" page.
2. Locate the order for which you need to issue a refund and click on the "Issue a refund" button.
3. In the "Issue a refund" form that appears, select the items for which you are issuing a refund and enter the amount of the refund.
4. You can also add a note to the customer explaining the reason for the refund if you wish.
5. When you are ready, click the "Issue a refund" button to process the refund.

Please note that refunds on Etsy can only be issued for transactions that were made through the platform, not for transactions made outside of Etsy (such as through a separate website or in person). Additionally, sellers are responsible for any fees associated with the refund, such as transaction or processing fees.

Blocking a Customer: A seller can't block a customer on Etsy. However, if a seller is experiencing issues with a particular customer, they can contact Etsy's support team for assistance. The support team may be able to guide how to handle the situation, or they may take action on the seller's behalf if necessary.

Dealing with Lost Packages: Etsy sellers are responsible for ensuring that their orders are shipped promptly. However, once a package has been handed over to the United States Postal Service (USPS), the seller is no longer in control of the delivery process. Any delays that may occur after the package has been handed over to USPS are out of the seller's hands. However, you still want to assist your customer in finding their package if they are unable to.

If your customer cannot locate their package even if it is showing as delivered according to the tracking information, there are a few steps you can take to try to resolve the issue:

1. **Confirm the shipping address:** Make sure that the package was shipped to the correct address. If the package was delivered to the wrong address, you may need to contact the carrier to have it redirected.
2. **Check with neighbors:** Sometimes packages are accidentally delivered to the wrong house or left with a neighbor. Ask your customer to check with their neighbors to see if they may have received the package.
3. **Contact the carrier:** Have your customer reach out to their carrier (e.g., USPS, FedEx, UPS) to provide them with the tracking number. Their carrier may be able to give them more information about the delivery or provide additional support.
4. **Contact Etsy support:** If you are unable to resolve the issue with the customer, you can contact Etsy support to help you investigate further. They may ask you to provide a tracking number, shipping address, etc.
5. **Have buyer contact Etsy:** If, after going through all of the steps above, a buyer still can't locate their package, I direct them to file a claim through Etsy. If tracking shows the package as having been delivered, Etsy will provide support directly to the customer.

Priority Shipping: While most sticker orders ship via First Class, if you are shipping large quantities of stickers to a customer and/or your package weighs over one pound, you will need to upgrade their package to Priority Mail. Priority offers the following protections:

- **Insurance:** Priority Mail includes automatic $50 of insurance for loss or damage. You can purchase additional insurance for higher-value items. Insurance will cover lost packages as well as orders that arrive damaged. You can claim these yourself or have your customer file a claim. Note that you will receive reimbursement from the Post Office with a check made out to your business name, the name you use on your return address. If you don't have a business bank account using that name, your bank may not cash it. This is why opening a checking account under your business name is a good idea.

- **Tracking:** Priority Mail includes tracking, which allows you to monitor the progress of your package from the time it's shipped to the time it's delivered. With Priority Mail, you will receive regular updates on the package's location and an estimated delivery date. This can be helpful if you need to know exactly when a package will be delivered or if you need to make sure it arrives by a certain date. In contrast, First Class Mail labels shipped through Etsy also have tracking, but the tracking information is not as detailed as with Priority Mail. The tracking number for First Class Mail will typically only show when the package was shipped when it was delivered or attempted to be delivered, and whether or not the package was successfully delivered. You may not receive regular updates on the package's location during transit.

- **Delivery Confirmation:** Priority service gives sellers the option for the recipient to sign a confirmation upon delivery. This service is optional and you can choose not to require a signature. Having a recipient sign for the package can add an extra layer of protection for you as the sender because it provides proof of delivery. But it could also be an inconvenience for the recipient if they are not home when the package is delivered, and they have to arrange for redelivery or pickup at the post office. I personally only use signature confirmation for orders over $100.

- **Delivery Time:** Priority Mail is typically delivered within 1-3 business days within the United States, although delivery times may vary depending on several factors such as the destination, the time of year, and any unexpected events like severe weather. It's important to note that USPS does not guarantee delivery times for Priority Mail, and delivery times may be longer during peak shipping periods like the holiday season. Additionally, delivery times may be affected by unforeseen circumstances such as natural disasters, strikes, or other events that disrupt postal operations.

Customer leaves you a bad review: If an Etsy customer leaves you a false or misleading review, you can contact Etsy's support team to report the review and request that it be removed. To do this, you will need to provide evidence that the review is false, such as a copy of a conversation with the customer or evidence of the transaction. Etsy's support team will review the situation and take appropriate action, such as removing the review or issuing a warning to the customer.

To contact Etsy support, follow these steps:

1. Go to the Etsy website and scroll down to the bottom of any page.
2. Under "Help" click on the "Help Center" link.
3. This will take you to the Etsy Help Center page, where you can find a variety of articles and tools to help you manage your shop.
4. Scroll down to the bottom of the page.

5. You will find a link to "Contact Support" or "Get help with a specific issue."

6. Click on that link, and it will direct you to a new page where you can select the type of help you need, for example, buying or selling on Etsy.

7. You will be asked to select a specific topic or issue that you need help with.

8. You will be provided with an option of phone, email, or live chat support depending on the availability.

PRO TIP: Fear of dealing with angry customers keeps many people from even starting an Etsy shop. However, in all my years of selling online, I can count on one hand the number of problem customers I have had. I am proactive in avoiding customer issues by ensuring my listings are accurate, that I package orders well and ship items quickly, and that I professionally handle customer issues. Even if a customer sends me a nasty message, I take a deep breath and respond professionally and do my best to de-escalate the situation. Do the same and you will keep any customer issues to a minimum!

CHAPTER ELEVEN: ETSY BOOKKEEPING MADE EASY

Let's be honest: Creating and selling stickers is FUN! Bookkeeping and filing taxes are not. However, Etsy sellers are responsible for managing their accounting, including tracking their income and expenses and reporting their earnings to the appropriate tax authorities. Where you file taxes depends on the country you are running your Etsy shop from.

You can manage your finances and taxes yourself using software programs such as QuickBooks, or you can hire a certified public accountant (CPA) to handle your books. However, even if you hire a financial professional to manage your bookkeeping, you will still need to do some basic accounting tasks on your end.

Fortunately, Etsy offers a range of financial information to its sellers to help them manage their businesses. This includes detailed data on their sales, such as the total amount of money they have earned, the number of items they have sold, and the average price of their sales. Etsy also gives sellers information on their expenses, such as the fees they have paid to Etsy and the costs of any advertising or promotional campaigns they have run on the platform.

All this financial information is stored and updated in real time in your account. From your Shop Manager dashboard, click on "Finances" to access the following:

Payment Account: Here is where you manage your payment and deposit accounts. You need to link your bank account with Etsy to get paid, and you choose your deposit schedule. Options include daily, weekly or monthly deposits. I have my money deposited into my bank account weekly.

Monthly Statements: In my opinion, this is the most important part of the "Finances" section. Here you can see your sales, fees, marketing expenses, and shipping costs, along with your net profit. You can view your monthly statements from the start of your selling account. Keeping an eye on your net profit will help you see if you are making or losing money. But remember that the net profit Etsy shows you don't account for your off-line expenses such as inventory and shipping supplies.

QuickBooks for Etsy: For a fee, you can sync your Etsy seller account with Intuit QuickBooks to easily track your sales, expenses, and tax deductions.

TurboTax for Etsy: For a fee, you can sync your Etsy seller account with TurboTax, which can make filing your taxes easier.

Legal & Tax Information: Here is where you will enter all of your legal shop information, which is essential when it comes time to file your taxes. This is also where you will be able to download your 1099 form at the end of the year, which you will need to file your taxes.

Fees: All selling platforms charge their sellers fees, and Etsy is no exception. Etsy charges fees to its sellers to cover the costs of operating the platform and providing services to its users. These fees include a **listing fee**, a **transaction fee**, and a **payment processing fee.**

The **listing fee** is charged whenever a seller creates a new listing for an item on Etsy. This fee is currently $0.20 per listing and is charged at the time the listing is created. Listings are active for four months and can be renewed by the seller at the end of that period for an additional $0.20.

The transaction fee is charged whenever an item sells on Etsy. This fee is currently 5% of the item's sale price, plus any shipping and gift wrap charges. The transaction fee is charged at the time the sale is made.

The **payment processing fee** is charged whenever a seller accepts payment on Etsy. This fee varies depending on the payment method used but is typically around 3% of the total transaction amount plus a fixed fee. The payment processing fee is deducted from the seller's account at the time the payment is processed.

Overall, Etsy's fees are designed to cover the costs of operating the platform and providing services to its users, while also allowing sellers to earn a profit on their sales. While many sellers scoff at the fees, imagine how much it would cost you to manage your payment processing and website hosting, not to mention collecting and remitting sales tax and syncing with a shipping provider. I'm happy to pay Etsy a small cut of my earnings so that they can take care of these things for me.

Expenses: As an Etsy seller, you may be eligible to claim certain expenses on your taxes to reduce your taxable income. These expenses might include:

- **Cost of Goods (COGs):** The cost of goods or materials used to create your items, such as sticker paper or vinyl stickers you order from a supplier.
- **Shipping Supplies:** Shipping labels, ink, envelopes, mailers, and anything else you use to ship your Etsy orders.
- **Office Supplies:** Pens, printer paper, notepads, and even paper clips are all tax-deductible expenses.
- **Insurance:** The cost of business insurance, such as product liability insurance or business property insurance. Since you will likely start your Etsy sticker shop from your home, ask your homeowner insurance agent about business insurance.
- **Services:** The cost of any business-related services, such as accounting or legal services.
- **Advertising:** The cost of advertising or marketing your

business, such as fees for promoting your listings on Etsy or running ads on social media.

- **Travel:** The cost of business-related travel, such as trips to trade shows or conferences.

These are the main expenses that most Etsy shop owners track. It's important to consult with a tax professional to see what other expenses they may note you can claim within your state.

Tracking your Etsy business expenses: There are several ways you can track your Etsy expenses to help manage your business and prepare for tax time. Here are a few options you can consider:

- Use Etsy's built-in invoicing and payment tools to track your income and expenses. These tools can help you keep track of the money you have earned, the fees you have paid to Etsy, and the expenses you have incurred in running your business.
- Use accounting software to manage your finances. There are many different accounting software options available, and some are specifically designed for small businesses or online marketplaces like Etsy. These tools can help you track your income and expenses, generate reports, and prepare for tax time.
- Keep detailed records of your income and expenses, such as receipts, invoices, and bank statements. This can be helpful in case you need to provide evidence of your expenses to the IRS or other tax authorities.
- Consider hiring a professional accountant to handle your financial management and tax preparation. An accountant can provide expert guidance on managing your finances and ensure that your taxes are filed correctly.

My Way: Etsy automatically deducts my account for fees, advertising, and shipping, taking these expenses as my gross sales and only paying me the remaining total, what they show me as my "Net Profit." Additionally, Etsy issues me a 1099 form annually with my gross sales. On my end, I only need to track my deductions off of the site, meaning I don't track my fees, shipping costs, or advertising.

Your gross sales are your sales BEFORE any fees or expenses are taken out. On Etsy, they will show you your NET profit after they take THEIR fees, advertising, and shipping. However, there are many more expenses you can claim as deductions when it comes time to file your taxes.

I use a basic spreadsheet to track my expenses every month. Every month I record my COGs, shipping supplies, office expenses, insurance costs, professional services, and advertising costs (Facebook ads and any enclosures I put into packages). Since I ship my orders directly through Etsy, I don't track my postage costs. However, on the rare occasion I need to take a package to the Post Office for postage, I will note that. I also track any mileage I may incur from driving to the Post Office or a craft store for supplies.

At the end of the year, I tally every category of expenses to get the year-end total for each. For example, I will add up my shipping supply costs for each month and enter that number into my year-end shipping supplies field. Even though I have a CPA who files my taxes for me, I still provide him with these expense breakdowns so he can accurately file my returns.

At the end of January, I download the 1099 form from Etsy. I take that along with my list of year-end expenses to my accountant so he can file my taxes. Easy!

Disclaimer: Every state and country is different when it comes to taxes, so be sure to consult with a tax professional in your area for advice on how to manage your own Etsy bookkeeping.

CHAPTER TWELVE: DAY IN THE LIFE OF AN ETSY STICKER SHOP OWNER

Sometimes the best way to learn how to do something is to learn how someone else does it. That is what this chapter intends to do for you as I will be going through a day in my life of running my Etsy sticker shop.

I sell individual 3" vinyl matter and holographic stickers as well as 3" magnets. For most of the designs, I offer a matter sticker, a holographic sticker, and a magnet within the same listing. All of my stickers ship for "free" meaning I pay for the shipping.

A typical morning begins with me seeing if I have any orders. I have the Etsy Seller App on my iPhone, which alerts me when new orders come in, but I process all orders using my desktop computer.

I usually wake up to a couple of orders every day. I will go to my office and log into my Etsy account, clicking on the "Orders & Shipping" tab on the left side of my computer screen. If the orders are for more than a couple of stickers each, I will print out packing slips. Packing slips make it easy for me to pull the stickers from my storage area, and it's also nice to include them with orders so buyers can see that they received what they ordered.

As an example, let's say that the first order is for two matte stickers, one holographic sticker, and two magnets, all in different designs. The packing slip prints with photos of each item, making it easy for me to match the products to the list of what the customer ordered.

After I pull the stickers and magnets for each of the two orders, I return to my desk and tackle packing the first order. I use clear self-sealing

3x5-inch plastic bags for my stickers, and I also include at least one free sticker with each order.

Using the example above, the first customer ordered five items. For this order, I would include two or three free stickers in their order. Sometimes I put the freebies in a separate bag with a "FREE GIFT" sticker attached, while other times I just tuck the freebies in with the stickers the customer bought. It just depends on the size of the order. I've had orders of ten or more stickers; for those larger orders, I put the freebies in their own bag.

For this first order, I doubled check the order on the screen one more time before putting the stickers and magnets into their clear bag. I also add in three free stickers. I seal the bag. I then fold the packing slip and tuck the bag of stickers inside, which keeps everything together neatly for when the customer opens their order. I put the paper with the stickers tucked inside into a craft envelope and weigh it. Let's say that this order ended up weighing over an ounce. When I go to purchase the shipping label, I will need to change the weight to two ounces, which is the equivalent of two USPS stamps.

I purchase the postage directly through Etsy and print the shipping label on my Rollo printer, peeling off the back of the label and attaching it to the envelope. I then put the finished order into my outgoing mailbox and turn to pack the next order.

After I have prepared all my overnight orders, I will put them out for the mail carrier. I then may do some research on what stickers I should create next. I use eRank to research shopping trends as well as just keep my eyes open to what is currently popular that might make for a good sticker.

If a holiday is coming up, I may start looking for holiday graphics that I can turn into stickers. Let's say that Easter is on the horizon. I will use sites like Creative Fabrica to see if there are any Easter graphics available. If I find a graphic I like, I will download it and then open up Canva to edit it.

After I'm satisfied with how the graphic looks, I will log into my StickerMule account and click on the "Samples" tab at the top of the page. I usually order a matte sticker, a holographic sticker, and a magnet for each of my designs. Sample packs allow me to order 10 of each style for only $9 each with free shipping. I upload my graphic and order the sample packs I want. StickerMule sends "Proofs" to me to approve before an order goes through. It usually only takes a few minutes for me to be notified that my proofs are ready.

If I'm not happy with a proof or want something changed, it's easy to simply ask StickerMule to edit the design further. Sometimes the graphic designers give me a circle proof when I wanted a die cut. It's easy to ask them to make a change, and a new proof comes quickly.

After I approve the designs and finalize my order, I may turn to listing new stickers. I have deliveries from StickerMule several times a week, so it's not unusual for me to have new products to list.

I also may work on my sticker storage. I use wooden boxes with individual slots that are designed for cell phones. They are used by teachers and other places where cell phones aren't allowed to keep them organized so that the owners can easily retrieve them. I find these storage boxes work perfectly for my 3" stickers and magnets. I typically arrange them to coordinate with the categories of my sticker shop.

I also have a case with small drawers where I store stickers I have a large supply of. If a sticker proves to be a best-seller, I will order a larger quantity than the sample pack and store the overflow in this box.

I have a list on Amazon with all the supplies I use in my Etsy sticker shop. Here is the link: https://amzn.to/3WJjARx.

I will attend to new orders as the day goes on. Any that come in after the mail carrier has come will be saved for the following day. I also try to share new listings on social media. And I pop into my Facebook group to welcome new members and post if I have anything new to share.

Here is the link to my Facebook group: https://www.facebook.com/groups/877482023647148. Note the name is "Jean Lee Publishing," which is the name of my sticker shop.

Occasionally I will have a customer contact me about an order that hasn't arrived. Almost always it is because the carrier scanned the envelope before delivering the order. I calmly reassure the customer that their order will likely be delivered within the next day or day. If after several days a customer's order hasn't arrived, I will direct them to open a case through Etsy. I do this so Etsy will handle the refund, not me.

My Etsy sticker shop is a fun side hustle for me. But even though it isn't my main source of income, I still take running my business seriously. I'm constantly thinking about new sticker designs, ways to improve my listing process, and how to better my SEO. I also remind myself that I need to stay on top of sharing about my shop on social media. Using my Facebook, Twitter, Instagram, YouTube, and TikTok accounts are all free and easy ways to promote my Etsy shop and sell more stickers.

CONCLUSION

A shop of ones own is a dream of many. But the commitments of daily life, along with the cost of opening a brick-and-mortar store make that dream out of reach for many. However, Etsy offers a way to have a store that you can run from home completely online. And for those who use and love stickers, opening an Etsy sticker shop can make the dream of owning a business a reality.

Whether you want to manage the creation of stickers from start to finish or you want to outsource the design and printing, there are numerous ways you can open an Etsy sticker shop. From planner stickers to vinyl stickers and every type of sticker in between, there are unlimited options for the types of stickers you can sell on Etsy. Hopefully, the advice in this book has helped you figure out not only what type of Etsy sticker shop you want to open, but also exactly how to get there.

My childhood love of stickers led me to open my very own Etsy sticker shop. Out of all the online businesses I have created, my Etsy sticker shop is the most fun! I love creating new sticker designs, listing them in my Etsy shop, and fulfilling orders. I love interacting with the members of my Facebook group. And I honestly love just looking over at my sticker storage area, enjoying seeing all of the stickers I've created and using them to decorate my own water bottles, laptop, and notebooks.

I hope you can find the same joy in running your Etsy sticker shop as I do in mine!

You can visit my Etsy shop at etsy.com/shop/JeanLeePublishing.

ABOUT THE AUTHOR

Ann Eckhart is a writer, entrepreneur, and online content creator based in Iowa. She has authored numerous books about home-based e-commerce businesses on topics including reselling, self-publishing, print-on-demand, and content creation. You can find all her titles at www.AnnEckhart.com[1].

1. http://www.AnnEckhart.com